Remorse isn't just simply another emotional aftereffect from having lost love ones.

Rather, it sadly serves as but one of the many constant consequences our hearts will be made to forever endure while we painfully struggle to survive our losses.

BET\/\/EEN
the
BEATS...

Is When Your Heart Speaks to Your Soul

GARY PERRIEN

Contents

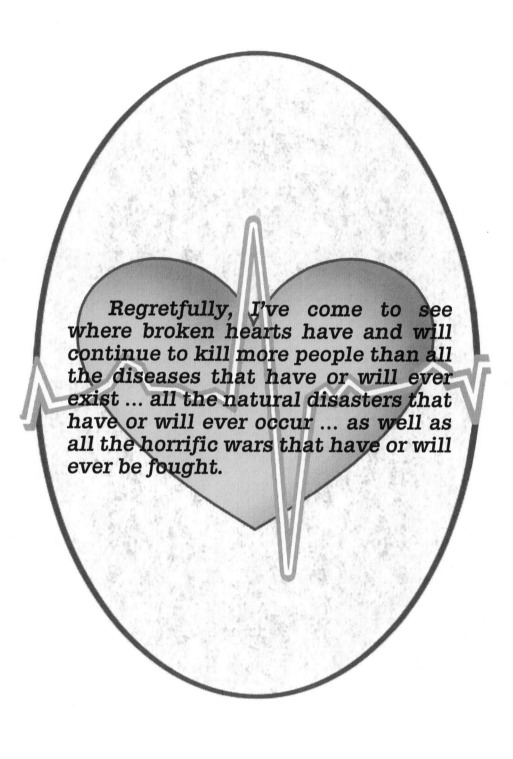

Regretfully, I've come to see where broken hearts have and will continue to kill more people than all the diseases that have or will ever exist ... all the natural disasters that have or will ever occur ... as well as all the horrific wars that have or will ever be fought.

Welcome ... My Friend

No matter how sincere we are about setting aside some personal and purely private time, it seems like something else always manages to take precedence. With that said, I'd truly like to thank you, in advance, for sharing some of your rare quiet time with me. I can only pray you come to view what's to follow as time well spent.

So, before you get started, I'd like to share a few things, and then, if you wouldn't mind, ask something of you.

Those whom I've trusted to read the draft of these writings often say how they're stunned to find my words not only reflect how they feel but much of what their hearts have longed to say. Ironically, it seems to please them that my words appear to be solely directed at their loss and with their love ones in mind. A few have even gone on to explain that my sharing how I got through such painful and distressing times has truly helped them to get through and beyond theirs as well.

Then, others often tell me that some of my writings are quite difficult to read because they stir up emotions they've managed to somewhat suppress. Yet, each revealed that though they must sometimes briefly set my book aside, my words continue to draw them back because of how they've helped them to recall so many things they prayed never to forget.

With that said, if my words manage to comfort or inspire you to view love, life, and yes, even death somewhat differently, then please let me know how and why. And if I've somehow moved you to better appreciate not only the love ones you still have but also those who've passed, by all means, let me know of this too. Then, if my words touch your heart such that you believe family or friends would either enjoy them or garner some relief, as well, please recommend they get a copy, or maybe just present them with one as a thoughtful heartwarming and moving gift.

Believe me, I truly look forward to hearing your thoughts and feelings, no matter what they might be, as to how you view what I've tried to both say and do. I sincerely invite you to send just as many messages as you wish, via my email: **TheAginCajun@GaryPerrien.com.**

For this opportunity and our time together ... I thank you.

Take what comfort you can in that the passing of a love one will never ever stop the two of you from quietly conversing.

For each time you speak, know that their spirit is anxiously awaiting to hear your every word ... sadly share in each anguishing thought ... and comfort the pain that silently seeks to overwhelm your tormented heart.

Just as we pray for them to forever rest in peace, they too beseech the Almighty to grant us no less.

My Journey

For you to truly appreciate and fully understand what's to follow, you need to first be aware of how all of this came about.

After receiving a call from my wife letting me know that my Dad had passed away, I knew if I didn't do something to occupy my mind while I made my way back home, I'd completely lose it.

To distract myself, I began to write down anything and everything that came to me. Initially, not a word of this was ever intended for another's eyes, nor written to soothe anyone else's heart, but my own.

Being so far from home, I had no one with whom to cry, grieve, mourn, or even talk. However, the good Lord graciously chose to intervene by letting me listen in while my heart and soul quietly whispered to each other. Much to my relief, he then blessed me yet once again by allowing my Dad to join in. As you'll soon get to see, that's when all three began to guide my tear-filled pen and have continued to do so ever since then.

These emotional excursions have truly taught me that there's no such thing as ever coming to grips with losing one's parents, or for that matter, any love ones. There just simply isn't!

I already see where coping with my Dad's passing will be like learning to walk all over again, but this time it'll be absent the security of the one entrusted soul upon whom I became so dependent.

Hindsight has also shown me that what I miss the most is that which I assumed would always be. So, I beg of you, please never take for granted any love ones that remain who can quickly and forever be taken away.

I feel the Almighty was very selective when He chose my Dad and Mom to serve as my lifelong saviors. Then, after they passed, He again opted to lovingly redirect our collective words, thoughts, feelings, and ongoing talks to become my eternal salvation.

I guess there are some, but I don't know of anyone that doesn't desire to leave at least some type of legacy behind. I can only pray the good Lord allows these memorialized spiritual exchanges to become that of mine.

So, take care, my friend!

Ongoing conversations with my Dad
that I can only pray continue.

Ferdinand "Ferdy" Perrien 1925 – 1998
[Photo circa 1942]

A collection of words, thoughts,
and emotions he has and
continues to inspire.

Dedication

Like far too many others, I failed to love, appreciate, thank, or even apologize to my parents nearly as much as I should or could have. Because of this, and so much more, I now constantly find myself trying to do so, albeit regretfully … after the fact.

Anytime I needed an encouraging embrace, answers to questions when I knew not even what to ask, or simply a supportive soul in which to confide, they were always there. In my younger years, even in spite of myself, it was with their unwavering love, ceaseless devotion, and insatiable tenacity that they somehow managed to keep me on course.

Shortly you'll be able to see how my Dad continues to inspire all that I do and write. Then, much later, once my Mom joined him, she too became an encouraging surrogate author as well.

Now, with the two of them back together, if you don't mind, these next few words are directed to just my Mom and Dad, but you can sneak a peek:

Everything I've struggled to express and have yet to compose, I dedicate to the two of you. Because you can hear my every word, thought, and prayer, I need not dwell on how much I love and miss you, although I know I will. I can only pray my words somehow manage to now touch your hearts nearly as deeply and profoundly as you've always moved and comforted mine. I regret that it's taken Dad's passing to provoke me into saying all I should have long since said. And now with you having joined him, my inexcusable silence will forever haunt me. Sadly, once love ones have passed there are no do-overs or second chances.

Even if just a small portion of what's to follow makes you proud of what I've tried to say and do, again, it is the two of you I must eternally thank. Though my delayed efforts began much too late, I pray my words will help make up for some of my faults and failures. And once the good Lord brings us back together, which I pray He does, I'll then have what remains of forever to say and do even more, and to love you both like I should have long before.

*My Mom's passing, over sixteen years after this book began,
caused me to somewhat revise this entry. Yet, the only
real changes are reflected in the depth, meaning,
and urgency my words now take on.*

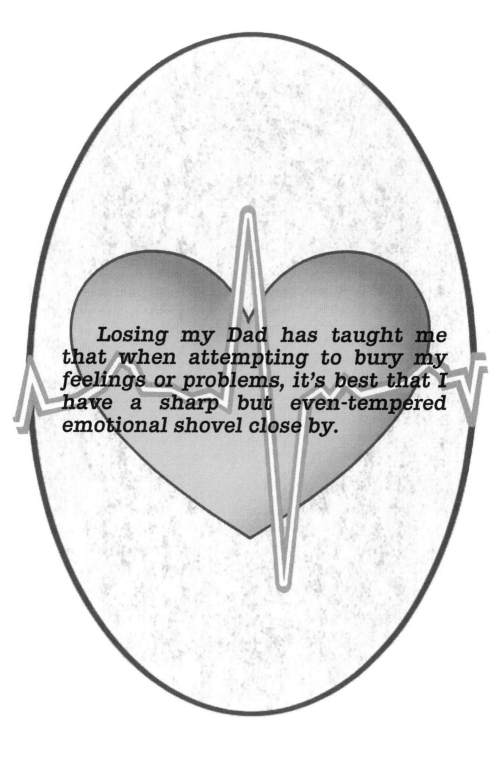

Losing my Dad has taught me that when attempting to bury my feelings or problems, it's best that I have a sharp but even-tempered emotional shovel close by.

My Dear Kelsey

As I've tried to convey, what caused me to begin capturing my most heartfelt feelings and thoughts came to me in a sad but rather unique and individually special way. More than anything else, that singular event not only changed my life, it formed the very cornerstone of all that I now write. Clearly, my Dad's passing serves as both the unseen source and driving force upon which my every word and action now depends.

However, when considering the proper usage of so many deeply rooted verses, there's only one soul that I implicitly trust with my words. Much to my regret I can claim no such credit, for it's her cleverly concealed efforts that grace and complement each and every page. Having spent so much of her time correcting the many errors of mine, she's truly a blessing the good Lord selected especially for me. Just so there'll be no doubt, all of the grammatical magic quietly performed in the background was carefully, yet caringly, orchestrated by my sole editor-in-chief, Ms. Kelsey.

What's so important is that this young spirited lady didn't just simply proofread and edit my first attempt at writing. Instead, she went well above and beyond to thoughtfully tweak my every word so as to fine-tune my heart's ultimate objectives. Then, if that weren't enough, she did this without ever altering the true intent of exactly what I first meant. Clearly, a bit of tender polishing by a thoughtful, caring soul can make even the most worn and tattered relics sparkle yet once again.

I really hope you decide to tag along on this journey to and through my emotional abyss. Though it would still likely be quite a moving voyage, if not for Kelsey you'd be traveling one riddled with grammatical faux pas and distracting, annoying typos. Somehow, not only did she fix things I didn't even know were broken, she managed to make it appear that this old "Agin' Cajun" can do more than merely place rambling scribbles and scratches upon a page.

Try as I may, I can find no words befitting, nor emotionally powerful enough, to express the true gratitude I feel in my heart and will forever have and hold ... for my dear Kelsey!

Gary

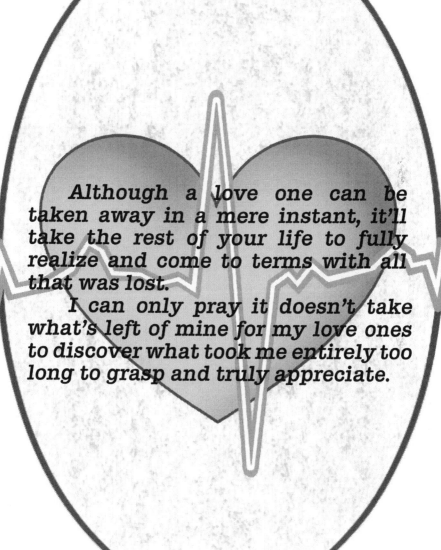

Although a love one can be taken away in a mere instant, it'll take the rest of your life to fully realize and come to terms with all that was lost.

I can only pray it doesn't take what's left of mine for my love ones to discover what took me entirely too long to grasp and truly appreciate.

So, here's where the journey begins!

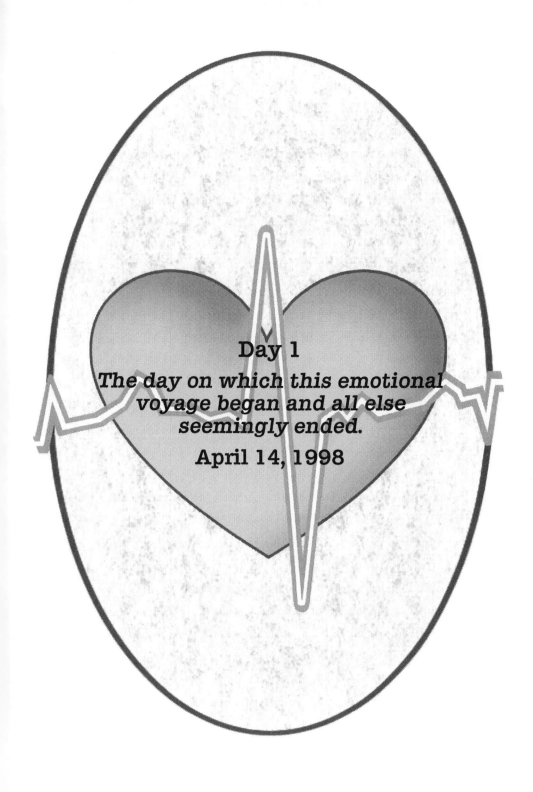

Day 1

The day on which this emotional voyage began and all else seemingly ended.

April 14, 1998

The Call

While I was in a meeting, a young messenger came into the room asking for me by name. After apologizing for the interruption, he nervously mumbled, "There's a call waiting for you outside in the lobby. I was told to tell you it might be urgent."

I'll never forget the look on that kid's face as I reached to pick up the phone, or even the sympathy hidden in the hotel operator's hesitancy to put the call through. Obviously, they were already aware of what I was about to hear.

The room where I stood was exceptionally cold and unusually quiet, with a rather stale, musky odor hovering about. The phone sat atop an old, deserted receptionist's desk in the middle of an otherwise empty elevator lobby.

Once Pat made sure that it was me she was talking to, her abrupt and total silence told me all I needed to know. Then, her quivering voice and continuing inability to speak further confirmed what I feared I was about to hear. Only scattered bits and pieces of words broke through as she painfully and tearfully struggled to say, "I'm so sorry … but your Dad just passed away!"

April 14, 1998 ~ 9:55 am (PST)
Stratosphere Hotel & Casino ~ Las Vegas, NV
Please bear with me as I attempt to capture my thoughts,
for if I don't do something, I'm afraid I'll simply
lose what little self-control I still have.

Dad ... I'm Sorry I Wasn't There

Though my heart can't find the words to speak, it's quite comforting to know you can hear and feel all I want and need to say.

I truly believed you'd be okay, or surely at least until I got back home. Please know that if I had even the slightest doubt you wouldn't, I never would have left.

How do I begin to explain how sorry I am for not being there for you just as you've always been there for me?

Dear God ... You alone know just how terribly wrong I've sometimes been, but never have I ever been this wrong!

If You would, the next time You're with my Dad, please let him know just how sorry I am and how much I love him!

April 14, 1998
Stratosphere Hotel & Casino ~ Las Vegas, NV
Waiting for a ride to the airport.
I can only pray my Dad forgives me for not being
where I needed to be when he needed me.

I know I'll have to be strong for Mom, and you can rest assured I will be, but what I need to know is who's going to be strong for me, for I know I won't be?

April 14, 1998
Las Vegas, NV ~ Airport
Clearly, I'm still struggling to gather my thoughts.

True happiness, much like true pain, are enjoyed and lessened, respectively, when shared with close love ones.

April 14, 1998
Las Vegas, NV ~ Airport
It's no one's fault but my own that with where I am
I have no one with whom to share my feelings.

Although I've lost other love ones, albeit it in my younger less emotionally formative years, having lost my Dad has totally redefined how I now and will forever feel and view what it's like to lose a love one.

April 14, 1998
Las Vegas, NV ~ Airport
To my Maw Maw and Pa Pa: I'm truly sorry it took something like
this to show me what I also lost in losing the two of you.

A Private Message to My Dad

There simply aren't enough words to describe, nor can I begin to even imagine, how I'm ever going to possibly live without you.

I pray you see the passion in my words, feel the pain in my tears, and always cherish the memory of the last time we were together, as will I.

Until that day when we're forever reunited, I pray that you'll talk to me in my dreams, embrace me while I sleep, encourage me when I falter, soothe me when I hurt, stay close by my side, and above all else ... keep me in your heart, thoughts, and prayers.

April 14, 1998
Las Vegas, NV ~ Standing in an airport check-in line.
Come on, people, move it ... move it!

If anything I say, try to relate, or attempt to convey to you about my Dad somehow reminds you of yours, I'm happy to know someone else is just as lucky as am I.

April 14, 1998
Las Vegas, NV ~ Airport departure gate
Just seeking some positive thoughts to help me
make it through till my next flight.

Sadly, and all too often, I found myself saying things I really didn't mean.

Then, there are so many other things I truly meant to say, but just simply didn't take the time to say them and can only now wish that I had.

April 14, 1998
Well, finally, I'm on a plane.
So, what else can I possibly say with there
being nothing left to be said?

Though I wish not to hide any of what lies hidden so deep down inside, I find myself praying not to become confused when it comes to conveying the very words my heart chooses to use.

April 14, 1998
With the countless times I've had to go out of town, never did it ever
cross my mind that I would dread going back home.

In Retrospect

I previously took great pride in being fairly capable of dealing with most problems, especially difficult ones. Then, earlier today I found out just how very weak, inept, and truly vulnerable I am.

My usual positive nature quickly eroded into an unstable emotional wreck, where I no longer cared if the next step I took would be my last. Regret and repeated second-guessing as to my inexcusable absence during my Dad's ultimate time of need became a nagging, persistent, and unwelcomed intruder.

Simple tasks challenged me in ways I knew not existed. Then, with nothing to do but sit and think, my mind raced at a maddening pace. When I tried to focus on something, really anything other than his passing, I became further entrenched in my grief. At one point, I remember forcing myself to look up and around just to keep from slipping into what I feared would become an emotional coma. It was then when I realized that allowing my mind to just ramble on helped to distract my heart. So, once I became totally engrossed in writing down the swarm of emotions taunting me, I finally began to experience a slight sense of relief.

I'm sorry to say this, but in my despair, I didn't even care if my plane ever arrived. This is not to say it didn't matter if I made it home or not, for I believe you know better. However, to make it there, I had to get through and past a place in time I'd never been before. What was I to do once I got there, and then, how was I to do it?

I prayed over and over for all of this to be but a bad dream; one from which I would awaken to find myself heading home, for absolutely no other reason than to just simply ... be heading home.

April 14, 1998

Do you think it would help if I prayed a little harder, and if so ... how do I do that?

Though life is often just as cruel as it is quick, seldom does it ever seem to move as quickly as it does when it's being so very cruel.

April 14, 1998

Finally, I'm airborne. As you'll see, I travel an awful lot. However, this is the very first time I wish I would have missed my outbound flight and remained home.

Dear God, please tell me, since you knew this was coming ... why didn't you just stop me?

A Permanent Hole in My Heart

Imagine how it would feel to suddenly find out you'll never see, embrace, or simply talk to a love one ever again. And for those who've already experienced such misfortune, my equally distraught heart weeps for you.

Then, for those who are yet to find themselves in that very situation, take my word for it; you'll begin to tremble at the mere thought of not having hugged or loved them as much as you could or should have. So, I caution you ... do so now while you still have a chance.

Believe me, if you wait until it's too late, a piercing sense of guilt will plunge a permanent hole in your heart that'll never heal and create an everlasting cavity in your soul that cannot be filled.

Both your faith and belief in God will be tested and challenged in a myriad of ways you would never have ever thought possible.

April 14, 1998
Dallas, TX ~ Airport
I just found a brief note I had made to myself that shows how
the closer I get to home, the more I realize how
very different it will forever be.

His continuing presence...

At some point, while I was jotting down these thoughts, my Dad let me know that his passing would not serve to silence him. In his own way, he let me know that he'll not only be here for me, but we can talk whenever, wherever, and for just as long as we please.

There should be no doubt as to his true presence, expressed in this and some of my other writings, for he's clearly come through on so many levels. As such, I left my previous entries just as they were originally drafted. Even though some expressed a tinge of doubt, I chose to leave them just as they are, for they represent my true thoughts and feelings at those yet still uncertain times. And even with all this said, I still feel more uncertain times are yet to follow.

However, if you're having trouble believing what I say, that my Dad is still with me, then just wait until a love one of yours passes away. That's when you too will quickly come to know just how meaningful their continual presence will be and how swiftly your belief in the hereafter and ever after will begin to grow and grow.

I genuinely consider myself most fortunate to have had the opportunity to follow in my Dad's footsteps in this lifetime, and I'll be truly blessed if I'm allowed to do so in the next.

April 14, 1998
Finally taking off
Thinking about my Dad and trying to
envision the future without him.

Just so you'll know, if you were to ever able to share just a tiny part of your heart with my Dad, he would have gladly given you all of his.

April 14, 1998
Just a little something to give you a better
idea of what I feel we both lost today.

Words can no more heal a heart that's hurting than can potions serve to soothe a soul that's searching.

April 14, 1998
Preparing to land
How can it be that I feel so totally alone though I'm
completely surrounded by so many people?

The solid ground on which I so firmly stood and relied upon now quakes and quivers beneath my feet.

April 14, 1998
New Orleans, LA ~ Airport
With the almost countless times I've landed here,
this one was like no other, for it jolted me into
the reality of what I must now go face.

Your heart alone will know if you're truly sorry or not. For long after you've already said that you're sorry, if you just can't seem to stop feeling a plaguing sense of how sorry you still are; then yes … you are truly sorry.

Then, if you said you're sorry knowing that you're not, maybe you might just be a lot sorrier of a person than you would prefer to think you are.

April 14, 1998
You can take this from someone who's
got a lot to be sorry for.

I Needed That

While waiting on my luggage, I met up with a truly good and long-time friend. I'm sorry to say, but I was unable to return the same sense of joy he expressed at our paths having crossed. Clearly, my heart, like my luggage, had not yet arrived.

Being such a close and dear friend, he quickly detected something was wrong and asked if I was all right. The best I could do was mumble, "Yeah, I guess I'm doing okay." Without a moment's pause, he then asked, "So, tell me, how's your Dad doing?"

Because he and I go back so far, he knew of my Dad's failing health. When I told him he had passed away just earlier today, he gave me a genuine, caring hug and expressed what I knew to be his sincere sympathy. He went on to say that not only did I lose someone special, but so did everybody else that knew him.

April 14, 1998
New Orleans, LA ~ Airport baggage claim
Thank you, my friend. Though I may not have shown it,
you'll never know how badly I needed that hug.

No amount of tears can wash away our worst fears, or lessen the sad reality of what's left behind following life's permanent, albeit sorrowful … ultimate finale.

April 14, 1998
New Orleans, LA ~ Airport parking garage
Though my words may help me to heal, they
also remind me of what's ailing me.

My sons often let me know, in ways I can't describe, how they respect and look up to me.

Since I too tried to show the same to my Dad, I can only now pray he saw and felt in me what I'm able to see and feel in them.

April 14, 1998
Well, I'm finally on the road and heading home.
Damn, I've become so automatic at driving this route that I'm
halfway home and couldn't tell you how I got to where I am.

So, What's Your Hurry?

Each time we returned home from summer vacations, my Dad would always take the same exact route. And the closer we got the more I would pester him with the very same question, "How much more we gotta' go?"

Yet, he always managed to smile and patiently reply, "So, what's your hurry, ya' got a date or somethin'?" In looking back, I see where he enjoyed watching me squirm while he waited for my usual reply, "Aw, come on, Dad!"

Here I am, decades later, and I'm going down that same old highway; heading home. With time to take a deep breath and think, it didn't take long before I realized that I was going home for a reason I hadn't yet come to grips with.

When I rounded a curve we traveled countless times before, I felt my Dad's presence just as if he were seated right next to me. For that one last time, I clearly heard him ask, "So, what's your hurry, ya' got a date or somethin'?" I caught myself wanting to blurt out my same old reply, but I didn't … I couldn't. Then, before I knew it, I found myself quietly whispering to myself, "Yes, I do have a date, for I'm praying you'll still be at Mom's when I finally get there!"

Right then and there, I saw a clear image of my Dad smiling just like I remembered as a child. Not only did this ease my mind for the rest of the ride home, but it blessed me with a final image of how I can now remember my Dad. His face, his contagious smile, and that ever so caring gleam in his eyes are forever etched into my mind.

April 14, 1998
Riding down old Jefferson Highway
Although I drove myself home from the airport, I was definitely not alone.

I see now how there's such a big difference between life not being fair and it being so very unfair. To not be fair is for another to not rightfully get what others freely receive. To be unfair is when something happens to another instead of one who's so much more deserving, and that doesn't necessarily have to be a positive thing.

My Dad was a good man. So, please tell me God, why did You choose to take him while leaving so many merciless and uncaring souls behind? And why not me … instead?

April 14, 1998
I'm sitting in my Mom's driveway and trying to muster the courage to go in.

Letting Go

The tighter and longer you hug a surviving love one, the more it seems to lessen your mutual pain; that's until you must let go.

Instead, you hug each other even tighter, all the while hoping and praying that'll somehow change the reason for your embrace.

It's then when you'll have to decide which to let go of first, the person or the pain, for you both already know that life will never be the same ... ever again.

April 14, 1998
Though I've embraced my Mom countless times before,
never did I ever not want to let her go
as much as this evening.

My Old Room

Not long after I had gotten home, I was drawn into my old room, where earlier today my Dad had last lain. How bitterly ironic, I thought to myself, since it was right there where I too once slept and quite often played.

Before I knew it, I found myself leaning over, tenderly stroking his now empty bed, all the while praying to somehow sense his lingering presence, but was sadly disappointed instead.

No cool breeze brushed over me, nor did I experience any heavenly glow, for the only thing that I left with from my old room today was what I felt my Dad wanted me to know.

I pray he passed on much the same as he lived, in a quiet, peaceful, and very loving way, with "Please don't mourn my death, but celebrate my life instead" to have been the last words he's most likely to have said.

So, in my heart, I know my Dad's spirit was with me in my old room earlier today, but since I forgot to thank God for blessing me with our private meeting, I will do so the next time I pray.

April 14, 1998
Something I just had to do and would have
forever regretted ... had I not.

As Today's Sun Set

With the end of the day finally drawing near, I was looking forward to some quiet, reflective time alone with my Dad's lingering spirit. Instead, all I got was more of the same, deepening the depth of my sorrow and further widening my span of pain.

Prior to today, I welcomed the setting of each day's sun, if for no other reason than it marked the ending of what was often a rather busy one. It also allowed me to temporarily set aside the many challenges and worries that cluttered my troubled and aging mind.

Yet, long before the setting of today's sun had even begun, my world had drastically changed, never to be the same. For the first time, I viewed the embrace of darkness in a much different light.

Never have I ever had to struggle so much to simply silently sit and reflect. My confused heart can't find the words I seek to explain my grief, and although my spirit carried me through the day, it too knows not what else to say. Then, with all of the unknowns that tomorrow is likely to hold, piece by piece I feel myself losing what little is left of my tormented soul.

As the evening progressed, all the fond memories I sought became a bit clouded and began to elude me. The clarity I once cherished was slowly being eclipsed, for I knew in my heart what was tearing me apart simply can't be fixed. So, I tearfully begged the Almighty for but a mere moment of quiet time where I could sit and enjoy some sorely needed peace of mind.

Then, just as if a warm, soft blanket had been laid over me, a vision of my Dad came through. The smile on his face quickly erased all the pain I had been holding on to. Though he spoke not a word, my aching heart clearly heard, "Please remind your mother of how much I love her and pass the same on to your brother. But, you can rest well each night, my son, for you should already know that my love for you, just as it is with them, will only continue to forever grow."

April 14, 1998
Well, I'm home, and dear God ... I truly thank You for blessing me with my Dad's brief presence, even if only to have been imagined!

A Brash Fool

When I went out to pick up something for my Mom, an individual I barely knew approached me in a way that I can only describe as being bothersome, at best. I don't know how, but he knew my Dad had passed. Instead of consoling me, he brazenly declared, "Hey, I heard about your Dad. Man, that's too bad. I know how you feel, but hell, before long you'll get over this just like I did when mine died."

Damn you, "... get over this ..." THIS! His words stunned me to the point where I was at a total loss to utter a single word that would even begin to describe the contempt I felt for this fool. As the seconds passed, his comments began to fester and further tear apart my now fully enraged and already broken heart. This idiot will never know how I feel! Obviously, he can't! How dare he say that!

Whatever his intentions were, he failed. It was all I could do to keep from blurting out some very befitting expletives to match his brashness. So, instead, I smugly declared, "I'm doing just fine! And don't waste any of your worthless time worrying about me or how I feel!"

April 14, 1998
I hope this "fool," and that's putting it nicely, reads this before
he approaches anyone else he knows to be grieving.

Well, I Guess It's Time to Go to Bed?

Though we've all said something close to this, usually without giving it any more thought than what it took to simply get up, place one foot in front of the other, and go crawl into your ever-faithful nest of solitude.

Prior to today, going to bed was little more than that, a way to bring to an end yet another often trying day. I also viewed sleeping as but a sign it was finally time to unwind and silently drift off until the sun arose again.

Then, there's today followed by tonight with neither being like any other. Never can I recall my room becoming so annoyingly dark and ominously quiet. I felt totally isolated in a place where peace and solitude once reigned.

I really didn't want to go to sleep, for I feared what I might dream and knew that tonight was nothing but a brief prelude to tomorrow, a day I prayed never to come, for when it does I'll be forced to face what I lost today.

April 14, 1998
Never before was it so hard to just simply lie down and pull the covers up.

Day 2
Knowing this day would eventually come did little to prepare me for when it actually did.

April 15, 1998

Mourning the Morning

I've never been one to sleep very soundly, and I knew last night would certainly be no exception. Silent, heartfelt prayers filled every tossing moment, interrupted only by morning's first light.

I awoke disturbed and quite unsettled, for I knew today would be the first time I would not be able to visit or even simply talk to my Dad ... ever again; well, at least not in person or in this lifetime.

Last night I found myself obsessively praying God would reunite us before the agony of today will have ever begun. I figured if He were to do this, me and my Dad could sit together and watch forever the rising of each new morning's sun.

April 15, 1998
Sorry, I'm not doing too good today, for I fear and know not what's yet to come.

Uncertainty

So, how do I do all the things that'll need to be done when there's only one thing that fills my every thought?

Being here for my Mom and helping her to get through what we must face today is by far my top priority. I'm hoping that once we manage to get past whatever we've yet to face, she'll feel a little less anxious and a lot less unsure.

Then, I can go back to praying how yesterday was nothing but a really bad nightmare that I can share and laugh about with my Dad come tomorrow.

April 15, 1998
Ditto from my last comment.

I realize those who care are driven to express their sympathy, and with absolutely no disrespect intended, I just wish more well-meaning friends would have waited a little longer before calling me or my Mom.

It's only now that I see where a love one's survivors sadly become members of a grief-stricken community whose friends, albeit with the best of intentions, innocently beckoned us to repeatedly relive what we prayed never to have happened.

April 15, 1998
I just arrived at my Mom's. So, now ... what do I do or say?

Tried, but Just Couldn't

Be it devilish or divine, I've always had the ability to pick just the right words and somehow make them rhyme.

Then, five simple words came to my mind, which I just couldn't bring myself to say, and I cried each time I tried to utter ... "My Dad has passed away!"

April 15, 1998
I'm with Mom at the funeral home making Dad's final arrangements.

The Hard ... Cold Facts

I've always considered myself to have what I believe to be an overzealous imagination. Even so, never in my wildest dreams could I have ever envisioned the hard, cold facts of dealing with death.

Love ones are made to endure a gauntlet of decisions engineered to test their faith, their strength of spirit, and the depth of their pocketbooks as well.

At a time when we are most susceptible to even the slightest gesture of kindness does an onslaught of devious commercial vultures come down to prey upon what little is left of the bereaved.

Knowing how grief begets sadness and lowers one's defenses do these mortuary maggots then descend to pick apart and feed upon our emotional vulnerabilities. They are masters at twisting what's not needed into necessities.

It's pitiful, but the passing of a love one has come to represent nothing more than an effective marketing tool for those who care not for the true loss of others. Though they bowed their heads, I don't view it to have been in sympathy for our loss, but rather in shame for their ill-gotten gain.

April 15, 1998
After dealing with the funeral home, if my words sound
somewhat bitter, it's only because I am!

Mixed Emotions

I now see where trying times give rise to conflicting emotions. And though laughter and pain would seem to be in conflict, both oddly serve an equal purpose with their results yielding different but sorely needed lasting relief.

April 15, 1998
I'm trying my best to figure out how to help ease my Mom's
suffering in a way that she'll understand.

A Parting Comment

While walking out of the funeral home I held my Mom's hand to help reassure her, and yes … myself as well. Then, just as we passed a room where I felt my Dad lay resting, to my surprise she asked, "Do you think Ferdy might be in there?" I paused and said aloud, "Hey, Dad, Mom wants to know if you're in there? I know it's gonna be hard but, try to take it easy until we get back tomorrow."

Then, to break the tension, and knowing how he liked to kid around, I chuckled a bit and asked her, "So, what ya' think he's gonna do with all this free time? You just gotta' know he's going to find something to fix, take apart, or tinker with!" It really felt good to finally see her smile.

April 15, 1998
And with a sincerely pleasant grin she quietly laughed and said,
"Hey, Ferdy … you heard that? He's you all over again!"

I Just Simply Didn't

I remember a particular day when I started to go spend some time with my Dad, but for whatever reason … I just simply didn't.

Now, the only thing I can do is to wish I had and forever regret that … I just simply didn't.

April 15, 1998
We're back at my Mom's.
As to the above thought, there are some things for which
there are simply no acceptable excuses.

My Dad's passing has set me to wondering that when my life draws to a close, will I regret more of what I did, or rather the many things I failed to do? By this, I don't mean things that are physical or mechanical in nature, but rather all the other stuff that falls on the emotional side of life.

Reflecting back on some conversations with my Dad, I now see that many of the doubts and regrets he both had and shared are also that of mine.

Yet, the one thing he made very clear is that all we ever need to fear is how what we did or failed to do affected others and not how it moved or disturbed us, instead.

April 15, 1998
Although I felt I should stay, I could tell my Mom wanted to spend some time alone
with my Dad's lingering presence, so, at her urging … I reluctantly left.

Steppingstones

Each time we perform a good deed or a true act of kindness, and we do so simply for the sheer love of others, we're assigned a spiritual steppingstone. And make no mistake; we'll need each and every one we can gather to get to the hereafter.

For every heart, soul, and spirit whose lives we've enriched, we'll be given another precious stone. Each time we tell the hard truth, we pick up an additional nugget, but for every lie we tell two are taken away. The degree of love, honor, and respect we've earned from others is the only thing that will allow our stones to be drawn closer together.

Then, in keeping with the overall body of our life's work, our stones will likely vary in size. So, clearly, it's important we do all we can, while we still can, to earn as many stones as we possibly can. And the larger the better, but beware, huge boulders are rare.

Those who've lived a good, fulfilled life will tread swiftly without the need to rest or step too far. And having collected more than enough stones, their journey will be straight and direct to where their departed love ones are.

Yet, what of all the other souls that remain? I guess some might have to step a little farther than others, as the life they've led has caused their stones to be small and scattered, but nonetheless, they'll eventually make it.

Then there are those who've collected only a few stones, and for some, maybe none at all. Since old habits for these tormented souls are so hard to break, most will continue to do as they've always done. They'll try to steal stones from another or simply tag along for a free ride. However, just like their forsaken, lonely lives, their old, ill-gotten ways will also have expired. This will leave them to forever remain at the very beginning and end of the path they've chosen ... as they are but one and the same.

Finally, spiritual steppingstones can't be borrowed and certainly never bought. The only binding condition is that once you step from one to another, your previous stone disappears. This helps clear the way for your love ones to lay their own sacred path. Then, once their journey to the hereafter is complete, they'll joyfully be reunited with all their love ones that were patiently and anxiously awaiting their blessed arrival.

April 15, 1998
I pray our stones are so close that they rest upon each other.

Wanting and Praying

The difference between wanting and praying for something solely depends upon what that something might be and how bad we want it.

To want something is simply to wish for something; nothing more. And I don't believe the Almighty listens nearly as close to our wants as He does our prayers.

On the other hand, praying allows us to emotionally seek His divine intervention for all that we could possibly ever want, even if it's something we can no longer have.

April 15, 1998
Yet, when there's something we want bad enough to pray for,
wanting and praying then become one.

Though it's heartbreaking to reflect upon how cruel life can sometimes be, it's even more unbearable once you recognize that it will no longer be as it once was.

April15, 1998
If this isn't reason enough for you to go spend some quality
time with a love one, then, I don't know what will be.

Could No Longer Go

Earlier today, the thought crossed my mind of how much my Dad really liked to just go browse and look around at tools and that kind of stuff. Believe me, if I had a dollar for every item he picked up and explained what it could be used for, besides what it was designed for, I could probably own one of those stores.

Then, reality set in and I quickly realized this was just another one of those places where he and I could no longer go and simply spend some leisurely time together.

As I drove up and parked, I thought of how here I am worrying about not being able to take him in with me, when it was at his urging that I went there to begin with.

So, after I finally found what I went there for, I did the only thing I could do … I walked around and spent some extra time so he could look at and play with just as much stuff as his heart desired.

April 15, 1998
Some places have special things, then there are some places,
for with good reason … are just special.

Words

Clearly, God never intended for our feelings to ever be analyzed or even thoughtfully scrutinized. For when a life has been torn apart by both loss and grief, mere words alone yield little more than short-term relief.

Then, with emotions churning in the pit of our hearts, ill-spoken words bring about disturbing doubt, giving birth to even more conflicting and hurtful thoughts.

Words can become powerful tools just as quickly as they can develop into cumbersome burdens. All too often it's not the actual words we hear but how they are said that moves us, rather than soothes us.

So, the next time you're moved to tell someone who's hurting that you know exactly how they feel, remain silent. Though well-intended, all you're really doing is minimizing their current agonizing sense of loss by comparing it to yours, which is clearly different and not likely to yield any comfort to either of you. I say this only because if your pain was still as present and real as theirs, such empty pacifying words would not have crossed your mind.

Words alone can't conceal or even begin to heal the pain brought on by the loss of a love one. This is why we need to be ever so mindful when expressing sympathy to another, for there are no words more important than those we choose to try and soothe a broken heart that's still slowly but surely being torn apart.

April 15, 1998
Westlawn Cemetery
I just had to come check out where we'd be laying my Dad to rest.

The Inner Trinity

Your heart hears you when absolutely no one else can and listens intently to your every prayer.

Your soul will speak to you when all others are silent, and gently comfort you by quietly whispering soft and thoughtful words of consolation.

Above all else, it is your strength of spirit that will nurture and sustain you through the worst of troubling and trying times.

April 15, 1998
As I stood before the yet to be inscribed slab of marble entombing my Dad's
crypt, both the reality and finality of his passing became all too real.
So, I went back and spent some more time with my Mom.

Balancing Act

Whether we like it or not, we won't be judged upon the life we believe we lived, but rather on the one we've left behind. And for those who naively think that there's a temporary middle ground in which to play, the right or wrong choices they've made is what will serve to determine their final score come judgment day.

The Almighty, while joyfully encouraging our hearts to remember all the good and righteous things we've done "for" others, has also seen to it that our soul has a very discerning conscience. It keeps an ongoing, running account of all the bad, spiteful, indifferent, or disrespectful things we've done "unto" others ... as well.

Ultimately, it is He alone who will decide where our eternal future will forever lie. However, before He does, He'll earnestly speak to both our heart and soul, for He already knows He can rely upon them for absolutely nothing else but the complete truth to be told.

April 15, 1998
I'm still at my Mom's.
Often, it's how and why we do things that's so much more
important than what we actually ended up doing.

Keeping the above in mind, eternity is often a double-edged sword. It gives us ample time to rejoice over all the good things we did, but it also affords us that same perpetual period to forever regret all the devilish deeds we so carelessly performed. In the end, all we're left with is to pray that the Almighty will somehow forgive or forget.

On the other hand, the one thing eternity absolutely can't and doesn't provide is any time to undo any of the things we never should have done.

April 15, 1998
Regret follows us like a menacing shadow and will only begin to
fade once our hearts accept the Almighty's anointing light.

Forever can either be our friend or foe, but I guess in the very end it'll all depend upon which way we go.

April 15, 1998
As long as we continue to regret what we can't forget, we must
devote much of our remaining time to mending our ill-gotten
ways if we ever hope to have any lasting peace of mind.

Day 3

I'm worried about what I might yet have to face, as well as all that I know I must.

April 16, 1998

How Do I?

How do I possibly get prepared for a final visit with an eternally resting love one?

How do I stop from seeking answers to so many questions when the only person I would have asked can no longer answer me?

How do I find the courage to go into a funeral parlor knowing the unavoidable certainty that awaits me?

How do I force myself to smile when nothing really seems to matter anymore, and with each passing minute, absolutely everything is becoming less worthwhile?

How do I convince my friends that I'm doing okay, and everything's going to be all right, if all my smiles are false portrayals and each sunset is but a prelude to yet another sleepless, worrisome night?

How do I simply get from here to there when all the roads I take seem to lead to nowhere?

How do I cope with these little, everyday things that heretofore meant nothing more, but now so easily tear apart what's left of my grief-stricken heart?

And finally, how do I begin to ever again enjoy some quiet, personal time? With everything getting so quickly eclipsed by far too many what-ifs, please God, bless me with some sorely needed peace of mind.

April 16, 1998
Waiting outside the funeral home with my wife and
sons for my Mom and brother to arrive.

A quiet gift...

As you may have noticed, some of my writings were drafted at a time when I wasn't yet totally sure that ongoing talks with my Dad would, in fact, continue. Trust me; I've struggled over this in ways words can't describe.

For regardless of the depth of your religious convictions, when you're at the same stage of grief as am I, you'll want, more than anything else, to believe that such is not only possible but likely to continue on forever.

With that said, I'll now cherish what I view as a celestial lesson I pray most of you will also come to accept and embrace, and not so much in due time, but rather, in and at your own time.

What I've come to see is how ongoing conversations with our lost love ones are blessed gifts from a loving God, for if you try to seek such solely on your own, that's how you'll forever remain ... all by yourself and totally alone!

Facing Reality

Thankfully, I've only been to this place a few times before and shudder to think what goes on behind its cold, concealing doors. And since I must now hesitantly face what I prayed never to see, please, God, if You would, explain why my Dad's death has come to be.

Did I do something so terribly wrong that caused all this to come about? For his passing has left behind so many unanswered questions and given birth to such painful, heart-wrenching doubt.

If anyone is to be punished please let it be me, for You and You alone have the power to set my Dad's soul free.

Clearly, learning to yield to life's misgivings, and having faith in the Almighty's greater plan, is the only thing that will get me through until tomorrow, in spite of all I might not yet fully accept or even understand.

April 16, 1998
Later today we'll be taking my Dad to his final place
of rest. The part of this that bothers me is not
the word "rest," but rather … "final."

Though the mourning process has a clearly defined beginning, it has no discernible ending, for it rises with each new sun and sets with none.

April 16, 1998
I always saw my Mom to be a strong lady in so many ways,
but I never realized how much stronger she is than me.

I remember thinking to myself, dear God, please don't let them close the coffin lid, not now, or at least not just yet, but they did.

The last thing I can recall seeing was the shadow it cast as it lowered across and over my Dad's face.

With the untold number of things I can no longer recall, this is the one thing I know I'll never forget, and I continually pray … I never do.

April 16, 1998
Clearly, of everyone in the room, I now see where
my Dad was the only one truly at peace.

Flowers will forever smell differently after today and never will I ever be able to look at them in much the same way.

April 16, 1998
Westlawn Cemetery
Take care until we're together again, and please
always remember just how much I love you.

It'll Be Okay

I now see that even when my Dad wasn't feeling all that good he had a unique way of making everyone believe nothing was wrong and everything was okay.

With my ability to clearly think, or even so much as reason, swiftly abandoning me, he quietly stepped forward to calmingly steer my heart back to reality.

He let me know that though many trying days are sure to come, he'll be right there with me long after the setting of each evening's sun.

This is why I now listen so intently to his soft and encouraging words. To be honest; I truly care not if you doubt what I say, for in my heart I know it's my Dad's spirit reaching out to mine in every possible way.

Then, as often as I can, I go off to find a quiet, restful place, where, if but for a solitary moment, he and I can once again share yet another warm, albeit mythical, reassuring embrace.

April 16, 1998
So, regardless of what's yet to come, with my Dad letting me know he'll always
be close by, my heart can now begin to both accept and trust in God's greater
plan, even if it's something like I said before, I may not fully understand.

Am I wrong for wanting my sons to always look up to me as being their ever-faithful hero, as I did of my Dad, or am I seeking something I've yet to earn?

April 16, 1998
In the clarity of a quiet, empty room, with nothing to distract me,
I see where the mind and the heart pose questions to us not for
the purpose of seeking answers, but rather to have us think
of things we should have thought of long before.

Until

Like almost everyone, I was somewhat afraid to die, at least until a few days ago. I had always been skeptical of the hereafter and viewed death as little more than my stepping to the other side of an eternally closed door.

Now, knowing my Dad is waiting for me, I no longer fear death as I once did. I've come to accept the fact that I'll just have to wait patiently while praying I go to where he is.

So, on that faithful day when my love ones also kneel to pray, I hope my words help to ease their pain and fear, and they too come to believe that I will be anxiously waiting for them when their time to join me grows near.

April 16, 1998
If I'm sounding somewhat confused, it's only because I am!

Dear Lord ... You gave me love even when I turned my back on You and had faith in me even after I lost what I had in both You and myself.

So, I need to know, if it's because of how I've been that You've chosen to take my Dad to punish me, once again, I beg of You ... please come take me instead.

April 16, 1998
If You'll grant me this one plea, I'll ask for no more.

Some Thoughts on Tears

Tears from a final goodbye, though wiped away, never really dry. Instead, they seep deeply into the fiber of one's heart, causing it to ever so slowly but relentlessly crumble and drift apart.

Unseen trails from countless tears are quietly left behind, leaving painful yet invisible emotional scars upon our tired and troubled mind.

What brought my tears to be was the loss of a dear love one I can no longer see. And although I have memories that'll never go away, a loss that lasts forever is a price that even the richest of souls can only but pray they'll never be made to pay.

April 16, 1998
Westlawn Cemetery
As we left the cemetery, I passed an elderly lady standing in front of a gravesite,
holding a small flag and weeping as she wiped her eyes. I wish I had stopped
to let her know that neither her sorrow nor loss was hers alone.

I can only hope and pray that the loving and thoughtful words my sons tearfully struggled to say during my Dad's eulogy will once again cross their minds when they pause to one day speak of me.

April 16, 1998
Just something else I need to add to my ever-increasing list of final wishes.

Mourning

Following the loss of a love one, we all mourn differently, some more than others and some not at all.

However, while thinking about this and how all-consuming the pain of our loss becomes, a thought occurred that now bothers me.

Granted, we've lost them; they're gone, but have they not lost us as well! If we truly have faith in the hereafter and that our departed love ones are looking down upon us, would they too not be grieving to see us suffering so? How could they bear to see us in such agony and pain without feeling much the same?

And, if this is so, then what does that do to the belief that our departed love ones are resting in peace? Is there a chance that this time-honored phrase might just not be as we would like to believe?

Well, I pray that Heaven is so good that once they're there the bigger, eternal plan of everyone being brought back together, forever, serves to sustain them.

And yet, when all this is said and done, are they not the lucky ones? I mean, who amongst us can say that they get to look straight into God's eyes with the coming of each new sunrise?

April 16, 1998
Though no one's loss is the same as another's and our pains clearly differ
as well, for when we hurt, we become one and the same, as we
struggle to get through our mutual living hell.

Our hearts feel so much more than we can ever hear or even see, and conversely, a lot more of what you'll not want to hear and pray never to see.

April 16, 1998

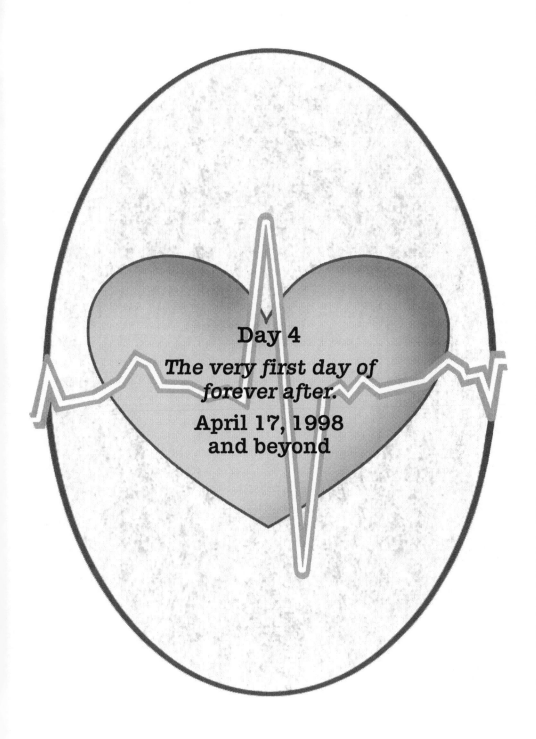

Day 4

The very first day of forever after.

April 17, 1998
and beyond

A Brief Pause

Now that we've gotten to this point, if you wouldn't mind, I'd like to take a brief pause. I don't know about you, but I need to slow down a bit while I gather my thoughts and rest my heart. Although it's been somewhat of a short ride, I believe you'll agree it's been quite a bumpy one.

I purposely held back the next few pages as I didn't want to initially delay you getting to the true essence of my words any more than necessary; especially in those first few trying days. I believe you'll agree that the very pigment of each and every word I write comes from the ongoing influence my Dad continues to have in my life.

However, before I resume, I need to properly and rightfully thank the countless others who've unknowingly helped me to get not only up to but completely through this entire journey.

Albeit mostly through chance encounters, let there be no doubt that it's their collective contributions that further helped to steady and guide my pen, for without them there's a good chance I wouldn't have gotten to where I am.

Good friends don't just tag along; they're there to help you carry what you can't handle on your own.

So, I ask you to kindly consider the following...

Additional Acknowledgments

With a humble heart, I wish to recognize the many others who played pivotal roles by inspiring so many of my writings. Some aren't even aware that they ever gave me cause enough to pause and capture our shared moments in time. Regardless of the degree to which they've moved me, how do I possibly begin to convey my deep and true appreciation for all that they've inadvertently but so meaningfully contributed?

How do I thank those who prompted so many things that may have otherwise gone unnoticed and unwritten? How do I incorporate them into sharing in the joy and pain that was brought on simply because we both experienced so much of the same? And what can I say to those whose names I don't even know? How can I let these caring souls realize they've not been forgotten? Please tell me, whom do I thank or acknowledge, and God forbid, what if I mistakenly overlook someone? So, how do I possibly begin to draw such a personal and vaguely defined, contentious line?

Every time my pen touches a page, or my fingers tap away at the keyboard, having my Dad, and later my Mom, close by my side allows my mind to roam free. I would think that by now you too have no doubt as to how all these spiritual interactions continually come about.

With that said, I alone cannot claim credit for words I must often reread to see what I had just written. Having so many helpful envoys, this book extends far beyond what I could possibly have prayed, or simply hoped, to contribute all on my own.

Well, it finally dawned on me that here I am struggling to come up with a way to somehow identify those who've aided me in my writing adventure when, in fact, I do so with each stroke of my pen. Anyone who has moved me to where I was compelled to reduce our experience to the written word, by either their actions or the very words they inspired me to choose, is undeniably as much a part of these writings as am I.

So, if you see, feel, or can simply place yourself into any of what I've written, I pray my feeble attempt at acknowledging you warms your heart as you've done mine. Believe me, I'm truly thankful that you've become a meaningful partner, even if you're not aware of doing so, in both my quest and this journey of our lifetimes.

Please read on...

So Many ... So Quickly

A dear and trusted friend posed a question to me I had trouble answering. He began by saying that he more than understood my mind being fully focused on my Dad's passing. However, what he couldn't grasp was how I managed to seize upon so many feelings, thoughts, and raw emotions while under such stress and duress. Beyond that, how could I draft so many deeply rooted expressions of both hurt and hope, so swiftly, yet so articulately? And then, to have so many shown to have been composed on the very same day, and at equally troubling times and locations.

Since my friend's inquiries had never occurred to me, I was at a loss to respond. I don't recall exactly what I said, but I do remember being unable to quench neither his nor my curiosity. Although his autopsy of my writing practices was polite and perceptive, the questions he raised bothered and provoked me. So much so, I knew that until I could provide him with equally befitting answers, my ability to continue composing would be hindered by a veil of uncertainty, obscuring and occupying my every thought.

From that point on, each time I was inspired to write, his questions would invade my thought process. Even though I know I composed every entry in concert with my Dad, again, my friend's earnest concerns and uncertainty continued to perplex me.

Is there some critical element of my writing process I've yet to recognize that allows me to do what I do or even the way in which I do it? My friend clearly deserved the answers he sought. However, for me to have faith in my future writings, I also desperately needed to fully understand how all that I'm inspired to write makes its way onto the printed page.

Then, while rummaging through my many failed attempts at replying, I realized the answer I sought lay right in front of me, hiding in plain sight. By going through my multiple notes and later trying to compile them into a meaningful response, I inadvertently recreated the exact same writing practice I had repeatedly been using since my very first entry.

Few of my writings ever come about as a single attempt; rather, my words evolve over time. When I'm driven to capture how I feel, what I see, or all that I sense, I jot down words and phrases on anything I can find that'll remind me later of my initial feelings. I've since learned to use my phone's voice recorder as it's so much more efficient and readily available. Later, at

some point, my Dad, heart, soul, and spirit all join together. It's then when we collectively convert my hastily captured notes and quietly mumbled thoughts into more organized, formally written passages.

(Continued)

Although our gathering to collaborate is sometimes delayed, I assure you the true essence of each entry bares the same exact scars and reveals emotions that remain unchanged from then until now. It's so reassuring to know that both my words and passions find comfort, and even mature, as they rest beneath the tip of my pen or sleep quietly within the confines of my many quietly composed, discreet voice messages.

So, I called my friend to explain the same reasoning I now offer to you and asked him the same as I now respectfully beg of you. Please don't view my words as being written at a given point in time, but rather as having been composed at a time ... with a given point.

Omaha, NE

Thank you, Jim, for your understanding, insight, and unwavering friendship. Gary

When least expected, fleeting moments of clarity arise only to quickly be overtaken by tangled bouts of sheer confusion. Conflicting beliefs ebb and flow more swiftly, more often, and so much stronger than all the tides that encircle all the lives I pray my words may someday come to reach.

Please know that nothing is any mightier or heavier than the regrets I carry for all that I've done and failed to do, and most of all, those lost opportunities where I, instead, truly disappointed my Dad. I'm terribly sorry for each time I didn't simply take the time to do as I should and could have.

Never the Past

Think before you ever say to someone who just lost a parent, partner, family member, or dear friend, and God forbid a child, that they must have truly "loved" them.

When attempting to comfort someone, please take care in choosing your words. Although you mean well, with "loved" clearly being in the past tense, your words may be mistakenly taken to imply that their love for them has also since passed.

Believe me, a heart caught up in the wake of a love one's passing is and will forever suffer in what to them will always be the present ... never the past.

My next entry will help to more fully explain why I feel this way.

Love vs. Loved

In my previous entry, I attempted to convey why the term "loved" should never be used when referring to a special "love" one who is sadly no longer with us, at least in terms of how we perceive the here and now.

Is it just me, or do you too find it odd that within mere seconds of hearing an old song or when tasting a flavor we had long since thought forgotten, we exclaim without any hesitation or reservation just how much we still love the simple things in life?

Since our deep regard and affection for the most basic needs and desires are not diminished by their mere absence, then clearly this must hold true for our most precious love ones as well.

Eventually, my taking this bold grammatical liberty developed into a true point of contention for me, and clearly, others as well. Whenever I'm questioned about my not using the proper tense, my heart persistently holds fast in spite of what criticism I might receive.

This is why each time I refer to someone that I still and will forever love, the spirit controlling my pen simply won't allow me to give in and use a word that applies to the past. When I express what I know to be a genuine, ever-present emotion, I believe my choice to be as clear as it is right and just.

So, when you see me use the term "love one" in place of its proper past tense form, "loved one," please don't view me as being wrong, but rather stop to consider just how painfully right I truly am.

Houston, TX
I seek not to change how you view this word, rather,
only to help you understand my use of it.

To not be able to bid my Dad a final goodbye is eating away at what little peace of mind I've somehow managed to hold on to.

Council Bluffs, IA
Which, by this point, I believe you'll agree ... there's not all that much left!

I'll See Ya' Later

Hey, Dad; if you'll remember the last time we spoke, I didn't say, "Goodbye," I said, "I'll see ya' later."

You wanna' know somethin' else ... that's the one promise I can hardly wait to keep!

Kansas City, KS
Please don't read more into this than was meant.
I'm simply thinking of when my loss will end.

Flash-forward to 2011...

Pat and I spent the entire day at the hospital with my Mom while she underwent some very serious, unavoidable surgery. Before going in, we engaged in some small talk, and even managed to have a good laugh or two. When her nurses finally came in, I gave my Mom a kiss, told her not to worry, that we'd be there when she comes out of surgery, and that I love her.

While heading to the waiting room, we got turned around and somehow ended up back in the same corridor as my Mom. When I got next to her I chuckled, "Boy, that was quick!" She smiled, waved her hand, and softly replied, "No, it's not over; not yet anyway," followed by a cheerful "Goodbye."

Before I could say anything, my Dad spoke up through one of her pre-op nurses. A young man, all draped in hospital green, who exclaimed loud and clear "No ... don't ever say goodbye; always say, 'I'll see ya' later!'" So, without any hesitation, my Mom and I both said in unison, "Well then, ... I'll see ya' later!" To this, everyone smiled as we parted, clearly feeling better and more positive than before.

I can't begin to explain how comforting and reassuring it was to know my Dad had just intervened, and at such a critical time. This was made even more special when I my Mom's nurse insisted we say the very same words I last spoke to my Dad: "I'll see ya' later." Obviously, at least to me, this was his quiet way of letting me know he would be in the operating room with Mom, watching over and taking care of her in my absence.

Two of my ongoing prayers were answered today: To see that my Dad is still close by my Mom's side and to speak with him but once more, even if it was yet by way of another.

June 25, 2011
West Jefferson Hospital
This was assuredly an unexpected but very
welcomed intervention by my Dad.

What Really Matters

The finality of death comes not with just the passing of a love one, or even long after we lay them to rest. Nor are all the tears we've shed just for the dead, as many arise out of the pain we hold inside, for their untimely absence will serve as an everlasting penance.

Our loss will become all too real each time fond memories are replaced by the loss we feel. Then, whenever we think of something we'd like to share with them, we'll cry all over again, as the love one we once took for granted is no longer there.

Then, there'll be those times when you just want to tell them something, anything, but they won't be there to be told. And, my dear friend, this same pain will surface yet again when your arms stretch out and they're no longer there for you to hold.

And each time we think to ask them a question, what we're really seeking is a comforting word from the love ones we miss and the voices we long to hear, as we silently pray for them to once again be heard.

So, no matter how many times we hear a familiar noise, we'll always glance around, for we're unable to stop our hearts from trying to find what in this lifetime can no longer be found.

If any of this has caused you to pause, and other love ones still remain, I highly suggest you seriously consider all that I've tried so hard to say. Then, go tell them just how very much you truly love them, again and again, and yes ... yet again!

St. Louis, MO
Trying to deal with what it takes to make it through just another day.

Death is never deterred by mere cries of loss or grief, but thankfully surrenders its warm embrace to those in need of such long-term relief.

Dear God, I thank You for ending my Dad's
suffering, and that of my Mom as well.

Each time I visit with my Dad, I see where it's okay to leave because I never really leave without him.

Death Itself

Death cares not for when you were born, your attitude, wealth, or lack thereof. It has no concern if you've had a good or bad day, treated everyone with kindness or disdain, and it doesn't honor your good deeds any more than it punishes your most egregious faults.

Death places neither value nor fault upon one inflicting the same upon another, for there are far too many murderers growing old in prisons while good and honorable people are dying much too soon. Then, there are the countless, helpless children, barely blessed by the breath of God, who fail to take yet another.

Death can't be bought, for the buyers are likely to be few, and for that which can be paid is too easily delayed. With good reason, death is both settled and collected but once, and at the exact same time and place.

Death is the only inevitable and inescapable certainty we must all face. Then, there are those countless poor souls who are taken away from their love ones for absolutely no foreseeable reason whatsoever.

Death is just as close as it is far and has absolutely no regard for whom you might mistakenly believe you are. And it doesn't care about who you may pretend to be, for the good Lord knows the real you and not just the one you want or allow others to see.

Death cares not how, when, why, or where one passes on; for none of that plays a role, or yields any advantage, as to when it becomes one's turn to be judged. Death is the ultimate mystery whose true secrets are only revealed to those who can then no longer divulge or share them.

Death is the only time when your entire life's work will be considered and truly matter. All that you've ever done or failed to do is believed, by most, to be what will determine where you'll spend all of eternity.

Death serves as a totally dispassionate escort to both sets of gates; one said to be above and the other below, with the one and only truly unknown in life being which way will it be that the Almighty chooses to let us go.

With that in mind, you might want to reconsider before ever saying or even believing that you have nothing in common with another. Though we may have differed here on this earthbound plane, in the here and ever after, with both empty hands and a fully exposed heart, we'll all become virtually one and the same.

This evolved from a really long discussion with a close friend about our concerns and beliefs surrounding the mysteries of death.

If Only but Once More

If only but once more I could gaze into my Dad's eyes to see them looking back at me.

If only but once more I could feel the hidden strength, warmth, and tenderness of his embrace.

If only but once more he and I could simply share a few seconds together, that would be more than enough time to both recall and relive an entire lifetime of lost and treasured moments.

If only but once more I could experience that same, unique sense of reassurance he alone gave to me. Then, maybe, just maybe, I could begin to look forward to not only the rest of today but all the tomorrows that are yet to come.

And yes, if only he and I could sit and talk but once more, oh, what a conversation that would be. Though I've thought time and time again as to what I would say, I have yet to figure out any words that could properly convey all that he has and continues to mean to me.

My God, if You could help arrange this, even if only but once more.

Omaha, NE
If you haven't already experienced the kind of loss that
would drive you to make these pleas, sadly,
there'll come a day when you will.

When you come face to face with God, are you going to be more in awe of what you see in Him, or instead, afraid of what He sees in you?

Houston, TX ~ Airport
Something to seriously think about while you still can.

I see my Dad's face in every cloud in the sky and his reflection in store windows as I pass them by.

He always seems to be smiling, looking right back at me, and for that, dear God, I thank You for blessing me with all I now get to see.

August 3, 1998
Houston, TX ~ Airport
Finally, here's something I can look forward to each time I travel.
Happy Birthday to my love, Pat, and yes ... I'm heading home!

My Final Request

You can speak well of me, but please don't bestow any unworthy praise, for my death, much like my life, will follow an inescapable maze.

And don't bother to assign nor try to proclaim either undue notoriety or unfair blame, upon these physical remains of what once was me, since I will forever no longer be.

September 21, 1998
Golden, CO
The shear resonating power of words rings
clear in more than just our ears.
PS: Happy Birthday, Mom!

After No ... Comes Why

Following the passing of a love one you'll likely find yourself repeatedly uttering a singular but quite profound word, "No!" And don't be surprised when the one word that's clearly defines a defiant reply quickly evolves into a tear-filled, agonizing plea.

With there being so many questions of the heart going unanswered and left unresolved, this small yet powerful word lays bare the depth of an emotion whose answer will take an entire lifetime to understand and even longer, if ever, to accept.

Then, once the reality of the truth starts to set in, the next layer of insulation we beseech is to ask, "Why?" Do you too find it odd that when we hurt the most we tend to ask questions whose only possible answers are those we prayed never to hear?

What eventually comes from our expressing these two small but rather descriptive words is like striking a flint against a piece of cold, hardened steel. For just as with the smallest of sparks, if left unattended, these two words, if left unanswered, will quickly consume all you once had and sincerely prayed never to be taken away.

September 22, 1998
Golden, CO
Here I am, spending a not so happy birthday totally alone while being really far from home,
but all it took was a quick call from my love ones to make it a much brighter day.

Faith

Dear God ... You know how in my younger days I never put much stock in organized religion. In fact, from a very early age, I tended to question and second-guess the very concept of aimlessly speaking to any form of higher power, but then my Dad passed away.

Just as seasoned wood yields more heat than green and each passing day succumbs to but another year, I now find myself constantly in quiet conversations with my Dad.

I've since come to learn and accept that it is You, and You alone, who graciously makes all this come about.

I'm not sure if this is appropriate, but I thank
You for blessing me with this gift.

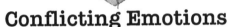

Conflicting Emotions

Well, today was just one of those days. I awoke feeling more unsettled than usual and troubled by a sense of loss that extended well beyond my Dad's passing. I can only hope spending some time with my Mom will help to lay my worried heart to rest, something she's always been good at doing.

Then, while still in that same frame of mind, I figured a visit with my Dad wasn't just overdue but necessary; so, I swung by for a quick chat. Though many of our visits are as different as two sides of the same coin, I'm never sad for stopping by, yet I always seem to leave with a sense of unavoidable regret.

Well, as it turned out, today was the first time I wished I had either gone later or even not at all. When consolation is what your heart so desperately seeks, absolutely anything that disrupts your emotional quest serves only to increase your anxiety, pain and confusion.

Within seconds of my arrival, I was met with an adolescent running wildly around where my Dad lay resting. While I stood quietly biting my tongue, I realized dealing with grief is like having to contend with a rude, obnoxious, undisciplined child, with the only difference being that one is young and the other is ageless.

This kid almost made me forget what I went there for,
but I managed to leave with what I needed.

To Not

To not be at my Dad's side when he passed away is to not have been where I needed to be.

To not be holding his hand at that very moment will haunt me forever, or at least till the end of my time.

To not be where the last thing I'd see was that he passed on peacefully, while looking right up at me.

To not be able to say, "I love you," or hear those very words grace his lips like so many times before leaves an empty feeling in the pit of my heart that deepens with every such painful, reoccurring thought.

Like most everyone, we've all had more than enough "to nots" in our lives. However, with these, in particular, wielding such a sharp saber of both grief and regret, these will remain high amongst my list of "to nots" that I pray God never lets me forget.

As bad as are my "to not's," my "should'a, could'a, would'a's"
aren't any better; in fact, being preventable
they could actually be even worse.

Through His Eyes

Each time I find myself thinking of and admiring my sons, I feel like I'm doing so just as if I were looking through my Dad's eyes. Yet, oddly enough, this is actually a self-imposed, bittersweet exercise, for it leaves me to wonder if he thought of me as fondly as I now see and think of them?

Rest assured, it shames me to say this, but for more times than I have excuses, I wasn't the son my Dad needed me to be. On the other hand, my two sons have always, let me repeat ... always been much more than I could have prayed for, or ever hoped to have been for him.

For this and many, many more reasons, I have yet to figure out why the Almighty so graciously chose to bless me three times over.

Monroe, LA
October 3, 1998
But thankfully, He has and, I pray, will continue to do so.
Happy 22nd Birthday to my son Craig.

It's Never Too Late to Love

Prior to my Dad's passing it never occurred to me to refer to a love one who was no longer with us as anything other than simply a departed love one. Of course, I missed them, but if the truth were told, their presence was soon replaced by their absence.

Although memories of them still lingered on, it's because I accepted death as something to be expected that their passing was much easier to mourn. I don't wish to sound cold and unaffected by their loss, but I also fail to see any merit in pretending merely for the sake of what others may think of me. If it's of any comfort, how I felt then has absolutely no bearing on how I feel now and what I've learned or come to believe.

To say I cared not if another tomorrow ever came says nothing of how little I valued the rest of the very day my Dad passed away. With my faith being tested, my heart proved to be terribly weak and totally unable to deal with such loss and grief.

After what I once took for granted was no longer there for the taking, I began to question everything. That's when I discovered how the demise of a love one not only clouds what lies right before us but places a dark veil over all that will forever stand off in the distance.

I've always heard "Nothing happens without reason," and "This too shall pass." Normally, I wouldn't have given such worn-out clichés so much as a second thought, but these simple words now give me cause to pause and more than enough reason to stop and think.

My Dad's passing has taught me that I don't love him any more than I did before, but oh how I wish I had shown it more. I've also learned that each time you're moved to say, "I love you," just simply say it without hesitation. Don't wait until either the opportunity or that special someone is gone before your silence and their absence become one and the same.

Denver, CO ~ Airport
Heading home for Thanksgiving
Just being able to spend another holiday with my Mom, my youngest son,
and the love of my life gives me all I need to be thankful for,
but damn ... how we all wish Dad were still here!

Lessons Learned

Sorrowfully, it often takes the passing of a love one to finally teach their survivors some of the hard lessons of life they're not likely to otherwise learn or experience.

We'll figure out various ways to insulate ourselves from the reality of our loss, but we quickly learn how going forward toward the unknown is as unbearable as is looking back at the past is inescapable.

Westlawn Cemetery
Choosing to go visit with my Dad is nowhere near as
hard as deciding when it's time to leave.

The difference between times well spent and times spent well will totally depend upon the cost we're willing to pay, or even forgo, for our allotted times together.

The real challenge then becomes ensuring that such times create memories sufficient enough to carry us through the lean or not so happy times.

Self-Inflicted

In reacting to a loss we're quick to build sturdy emotional walls to keep what's left of our lives from caving in on us, and corral all that we believe to be good close by.

However, more often than not, all we really do is erect barriers that fence out our remaining love ones and create obstacles that hold ourselves back from healing.

December 24, 1998
Lake Charles, LA
Well, at least I'll be home for Christmas by tomorrow.

As comforting as it is to believe that my Dad can now hear every word I think or feel, this sometimes scares me even more.

December 25, 1998
Spending Christmas at my Mom's.
This being the first Christmas without my Dad, though we really tried
we soon realized it will never, ever be the same. Merry Christmas,
Dad, and know that we all love and miss you so very much!

Lost Opportunities

Looking back, regretfully, my Dad and I never talked quite as much as we could or should have. You know what I mean: really sat down and just talked, one on one.

Now that he's gone, it's so reassuring to be able to talk with him anytime, anywhere, and for just as long as our hearts choose to.

If that weren't enough, what's even more comforting is to know that he'll always be patiently waiting to listen to whatever I have to say.

I'm just so sorry that it's only now I've come to see how I failed to take the time, while there was still some, to do this and even more. Now, to simply say I'm sorry doesn't even begin to explain the depth of my sorrow!

January 12, 1999
It's only through the love of God that my Dad and I can now start to
recapture the many opportunities we lost and let pass us by.
Happy Birthday, Dad!

Wishes and Prayers

We make wishes for all the things that money can easily buy, but prayers come from deep down within for the many other things that only a loving God can supply.

I believe you'll agree that at one time or another, we're all guilty
of abusing and misusing both of these desires.

Me

I now see and feel so much of my Dad in me, and many friends tell me they see a lot of me in my sons.

Then, why might it be that no one ever seems to see the me in me?

So, if you would, please tell me what it might be
that you seem to think you see in me?

An Unexpected Reaction

Recently, while attending a friend's funeral, I found myself talking with a mixed group of people. One of them, apparently much closer to my departed friend than I, passed a remark that literally confounded all of us. When she turned to look at JJ, she mumbled something to the effect, "I really envy him. He's so fortunate to now be with his love ones rather than being stuck here with us!"

Clearly, this brought all other conversations to a screeching halt, leaving us in a virtual collective state of confusion. Now visibly upset, she paused and further said, "It must be nice to never have had a spouse or kids to lose!" To that, a rather young girl standing next to her slowly shook her head, quietly moaned, and abruptly left. Before she turned to walk away, you could see tears that had been held back for far too long forming in her eyes. After making a quick, yet painfully disguised reference as to the young girl being her daughter, our troubled friend left as well.

With not knowing her, I couldn't tell if she was serious or being remorsefully sarcastic as a few of our group also softly wondered aloud what could have brought that on.

It was then when one of the ladies in our group opted to explain her friend's actions. She shared that she had lost her husband about a year ago following a long, drawn-out illness, and her only son in an auto accident just a few weeks back. Hearing this, an overwhelming sense of sympathy quickly erased any doubt I had as to her reasons for feeling as she does. I can only pray it's not in the good Lord's plans for me to ever suffer through anything even close to what she's had to bear.

Long after my friend's services were over, I couldn't get this lady, her daughter, their horrific set of circumstances, or her troubling words to stop haunting me. Clearly, she was quietly crying out for the kind of help we were sadly ill-prepared to provide her.

When losing love ones to the degree this poor soul has been made to endure, time becomes all-consuming. It's no longer simply a matter of making it from week to week, or even day to day; it's reduced to merely getting through one moment to the next.

Houston, TX
I'm sorry to say this, but with grief being such an overwhelming and all-consuming emotion, I can only pray she and her daughter somehow manages to find some peace ... sometime soon.

A Flower's Gift

I truly believe flowers
not only sense the
presence of love

but joyfully return
it as well.

For each time I visit
with my Dad, they
greet me with a

smile, bathe in my
tears, and try as
best they can to
reassure me that when I
leave they'll be there
for him in my absence.

Westlawn Cemetery
When I stopped by to visit with my Dad, one of them was
kind enough to let me know just how lovingly
he speaks of me between our visits.

With sorrow too deep for mere words to express, and deafening sighs that can't be heard, it's so comforting now to know when I speak with my Dad, I need not say a word.

To know I'm no longer restricted by mere words to express all that I
feel allows me to also now feel without any restrictions.

How close is close and how far is far, with the only answer to this being the distance between where you and your love ones are.

But then, we have memories which cross over and draw together both time and space, blessing us with heart-soothing recollections that are purely an act of a loving God's continual, redeeming grace.

Not everything has a scale by which it can be measured.

Yes, I'm ashamed to admit this, but it's only now that I see how my emotions for my Dad seem to be more intense since he's passed than they were when I could still have expressed them.

Though my deep feelings of guilt are well warranted by what was clearly my fault, I refuse to use this as an excuse, but rather view it as a sign from my Dad of what I must correct, while I still can, for the sake of my Mom.

Once again, my Dad brings clarity to when and where it's needed.

Heading Home

For those who travel as much as I do, just the mere thought of going home helps to make long and arduous trips almost palatable. Hectic, impatient airport crowds neither bothered nor irritated me, and I tend to view waiting for connecting flights to be just a necessary inconvenience. However, none of this was the case one year ago today.

Shuttle buses weren't moving fast enough, and ticket lines were unusually long. My patience was tried, tested, and strained in ways I would not wish on anyone. What I normally took in stride became what seemed like insurmountable problems directed solely at me. I knew today would be difficult, but I never envisioned it to be this bad!

Then, finally with little time to do anything but sit and reflect, I couldn't come to grips with my dire urgency to get home. The reality of knowing what awaited me was too much to bear, and I found myself on the **1 Year** verge of uncontrollably losing it.

It was then when my Dad spoke to me through another, and all else went silent except for a very lonely-sounding voice coming seemingly from out of nowhere. "Damn!" the voice cried out, "I can't believe I'm going home. I can hardly wait to see my Mom and Dad!"

For that very brief moment, both my heart and time truly stopped. In so few words this stranger halted my fears, brought me back into focus, and set free every emotion that was violently churning within me. She was looking forward to the one thing I could not bring myself to face, the sad reality of a love one's mortality.

Unknowingly, this young lady made perfectly clear all I needed to hear. I too was heading home, and not to just be with my Mom but to visit with my Dad as well.

April 14, 1999
Dallas, TX ~ Airport
I can't believe it's already been a year and here I am, yet again, heading home, sitting in the same airport, the same concourse, with the same feelings, and for all the very same reasons.

Between the Beats... Is When Your Heart Speaks to Your Soul

I can't begin to tell you how much I truly anguished over coming up with not just an appropriate title, but one that would also emotionally address all that I've tried so hard to convey.

Well, earlier today, after a rather long visit with my Dad, I sat in my car and pondered over the quiet intensity of our visits and ongoing talks. It was then when it occurred to me that it's not just the time we spiritually spend together; rather, it's how we stay connected through the beating of our hearts, even though we're seemingly so far apart.

The level of pain and grief I felt during that emotionally overpowering moment was overtaken by the chills I had when I softly whispered these very poignant words to myself as I quietly sat in my car. I knew right then and there that this was my Dad's way of letting me know he was happy with my choice. I can only hope you are as well.

May 1, 1999
Westlawn Cemetery
I would like this title to be my epitaph.

I will never be more of the person I truly am than in that very second my feet hit the floor each morning.

For as soon as I start thinking about who, how, or what I need to be, do I then morph into the person I half-heartedly allow others see, albeit someone I know, in so many ways, is not the real me ... I would rather they see.

Denver, CO ~ Airport
I can't explain why, but in watching a father sternly correcting his young son this thought
oozed from my pen. I can only hope this young soul will one day realize just how
very lucky he is to have had a father who clearly loves him so very much.

Don't Thank Me

With my Dad now always by my side, there are two things I can look forward to and rely upon. First, I'm never truly alone. Secondly, it's during these times we spend together that words and thoughtful expressions just seem to come to me.

Each time I'm driven to write, my Dad's spirit nuzzles up close to mine, and then between the two of them do words, like these, upon each page just seem to glide.

Please know that it is their collective wisdom, words, and thoughts that ooze out of my pen; never are they ever mine alone.

So, remember, if you're truly moved by anything I've penned, then it is absolutely the two of them you'll need to thank ... if or when you get to "The End."

Salt Lake City, UT
It's only right that credit be given not only
where it's due but in how it's earned.

There are times when life isn't what we wanted, expected, or prayed for it to be, and the light at the end of our tunnel often becomes so very dim it's almost impossible to even see.

Though our hearts are sometimes weighted down with far too much for us to bear, we must remember that at some point our love ones will also be hurting just the same, when we too are no longer there.

Kansas City, KS
I realize this is quite selfish, but as much as I still miss
and need my Dad, I pray my love ones continue
to miss and need me as much as I do him.

Listen closely to the anguishing cries of your heart and wisely surrender to the desires of your soul but fail not to heed the advice and counsel of your spirit.

Together they will guide, comfort, and support you even when all others seem to have abandoned you.

San Antonio, TX
Though it's consoling to trust in your heart and reassuring to follow your soul,
it's your spirit that will forever protect and guide you.

From a Father's Point of View

It's only now that I've learned from my own life's experiences one of the many wishes my Dad must have surely had.

Like him, I can only pray my sons come to see and appreciate me for who and what I truly am, sometime soon, and not after it's too late for us to share that bond.

September 22, 1999
Omaha, NE
Just another self-centered rambling thought, while far away from home,
because yet again, here I am ... spending my birthday all alone.

At some point, each time while I'm returning home I think of my Dad no longer being there. This time, a rather odd, some might think troubling, thought came to mind.

I wondered how it might be to have my Dad back with me, but when it came time for him and the Almighty to leave again, would they then take me back with them?

Omaha, NE ~ Airport

False Promises

When faced with the possibility of losing someone very dear to you, you'll find yourself reciting what in your heart you believe to be promises to God.

You'll freely commit to never again doing any of the not so nice things you did before and immediately pledge to start doing everything you should have already done, and even more.

However, please don't be foolish enough to think that your empty oaths are being offered up to God; rather, what you're really doing is mistakenly cutting shameful deals with the devil.

Make no mistake, God already knows exactly what you will and won't do ... even in the worst of trying and troubling times!

October 3, 1999
Salt Lake City, UT
Might I suggest you remember this when you too
are faced with the same fate as was I.
PS: Happy Birthday to my son Craig.

A Polite Request

As I somewhat considered earlier, I realize it's quite inappropriate to ever consider demanding anything of the Almighty, even if I were to do so with the very best and sincerest of intentions.

So, dear Lord, please forgive me, yes ... yet again, but I'll be eternally grateful if You would either give my Dad back to me or just come take me to him!

Believe me, I'd prefer the first, but whichever
You choose will suit me just fine.

It's taken me this long to finally come to grips with and appreciate the depth of frustration my Dad must surely have experienced during my younger, more formative years.

I can only thank God that He chose to complement the warmth of my Dad's devoted love and compassion with clearly an overabundance of both tolerance and relentless understanding.

St. Louis, MO
A silent and long, long overdue apology to my Dad,
but how do I begin to say I'm sorry when I don't
even know where I should begin?

I've heard it said that children are made to pay for the sins of their fathers. Then, if this is so, what of those who are as fortunate as I am to not have such a fate to suffer? Is it possible that the Almighty graciously chose to bless us with some of their many talents, instead?

Reno, NV
And for this I thank the both God and my Dad.

I can't help but wonder, why would anyone ever concern themselves with mourning a love one's absence if they've never celebrated their presence?

December 25, 1999
Tonight, Mom and I will celebrate my Dad's memory, his continuing presence,
and hopefully a bit of Christmas as well.
Merry Christmas, Dad!

When confronted with the depth of another's pain, be mindful that it's only through the grace of a benevolent God that you too are not suffering much the same.

Avondale, LA
A long-time friend just recently told me of losing his only son,
who was in the Air Force, as is our youngest.

Nothing eats away at your heart, soul, and spirit more than the hurt you hold inside.

Avondale, LA
The fear, pain, and anguish I saw in my friend's eyes remind me
of how my own heart feels each time our son tells us
he's being deployed to some foreign land.

Don't pile up any more anger, resentment, hurt, or hatred than you can bear to drag around with you everywhere you go.

Avondale, LA
A bit of wisdom that took me too long to learn, and which I pray
my friend soon comes to understand as well.

The pain we hold inside is not all that much different than what we allow others see, it just differs in its degree.
We learn quick how much it hurts to try and hide what can't be hidden.

Though it's been well over a month, all the fears I have for my son won't
allow me to stop worrying about my friend and the loss of his son.

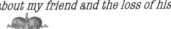

While the closeness of others will obviously serve to soothe your heart following the loss of a love one, when they're nowhere around or they can't be found, your strength of spirit and faith will carry you through.

So, take care of yourself, my friend.

Choices

We all do things when we're young and foolish that cause most of us to feel guilty; some right then and there, and others only after being caught. Yet there are some that manage to go through life feeling totally unaffected, expressing neither guilt nor shame.

I believe those who aren't moved to make amends only have but two choices: Either do nothing and continue to pretend as if all their wrongdoings are easy to forget; or start doing the right thing, and avoid a life that they'll eventually, in the here and ever after, truly come to regret.

The Hurt Won't Last

Sadly, there will come a time when your heart will ache so badly that nothing else will seem to matter.

Your emotions will teeter between giving up and giving in. And all attempts by love ones to comfort and console you will be silenced by the ever-present pain of your loss.

As hard as it may be, try your best to hold on, for from here on, **2 Years** you'll never be alone.

In the meantime, you can rest assured that your spirit is compassionately hovering close by ready to dry your tears, warm your heart, and embrace you when no one else is near.

When needed, your soul will help you bear the agony you alone cannot carry, for it knows that suffering is but a part of the healing process and that the hurt won't last as long as will your loss.

April 14, 2000
Westlawn Cemetery
Losing my Dad has set me on a new path to which I can see no end, or at least not until I too arrive at mine when he and I can then embrace, yet once again.

If you ever lose something that's as near and dear to you as life itself, don't even bother trying to look for it in this lifetime.

Westlawn Cemetery
Really, think about it. Where would or could you even begin to look?

True Gifts

If you could fly, would you not gracefully spread your wings and soar aimlessly every chance you have? And how nice would it be, even but for a brief moment, to rise high above and escape all the madness we earthbound souls are destined to endure? Then, if you could fly, would you ever chance coming back down?

Then, if you could sing, would you not hum along with hummingbirds and harmonize with every passing nightingale? And how could you possibly let a single day go by without sharing a caring melody with another's equally loving heart?

And if you could, simply by your touch, heal the sick, or just ease another's pain, would you not tenderly caress and lovingly embrace each and every troubled soul or hurting heart that crossed your path?

So, if you could somehow do all these things ... how could you not?

Fort Worth, TX
The good Lord, in His ultimate and infinite wisdom, has bestowed
certain gifts only upon those worthy of bearing them.

Ahhhh

Ailing as much as I have been lately, I see what my Dad meant when, at times, he felt so bad, he would hurt all over. I'm also beginning to understand how it becomes easier, almost comforting, to consider giving up rather than continuing to fight the pain any longer.

When I'm hurting like that, what helps to comfort me more than anything else is to quietly sigh ever so deeply and let it out ever so softly, just like I heard my Dad do so many times. For like him, I too wish not to give my love ones a reason to become unnecessarily concerned.

I also do this because each time I sigh the same as he did, the sound I make reminds me of exactly what he sounded like. And there's absolutely nothing else that makes me feel better than to hear what it sounds like to still have my Dad so near.

Dallas, TX
And, yes ... it feels that good!

Absolutely Nothing ... Is That Important

My Dad usually kept himself pretty busy. So, it wasn't that often he had time to just pop in for a visit, especially in the middle of the afternoon. Well, there's a particular day when he did just that, which I'm compelled to share with you, and, I'm sorry to say, you'll see why.

I had drafted an extremely important work-related document, which had to be postmarked no later than the end of the very next business day. As such, late that night and early the next morning, I began editing and making all the necessary corrections to complete the project.

Then, while I was proofreading the final draft, my Dad stopped by to visit. Well, after we'd been sitting in the living room for quite a while, I asked if he wouldn't mind coming to talk with me in my office so I could finish what I was doing. We actually had what I felt to be some really good, ongoing conversations, and even managed to laugh a time or two. In spite of this, in hindsight, I now see where I selfishly failed him, and miserably so!

All the signs were there; and believe me, this is both a poor reason and even worse excuse, but I was just too damn busy to acknowledge them. Between the faraway look I remember seeing in his eyes and the hesitation I heard in his voice, I should have known he had more to say to me. Instead, sensing my urgency to finish, he sacrificed his own desire to stay by saying he had somewhere else to go and we'd talk later. He left because to him that was the right thing to do; that's just simply how my Dad was.

With that said, what is and will forever be unforgivable is that I allowed him to leave. I've long since forgotten what I had been working on, but what I will never forget is that I didn't take the time to set aside whatever I was doing. For had I, he would have stayed and share the burden I now know he was carrying and wanting to divulge.

It wasn't until days later when I found out he had come by to tell me that his prostate cancer was showing signs of returning. Knowing what he knew then but didn't reveal haunts me in ways that few other memories can or ever will. Take this however you wish, but I've asked the good Lord that I be made to walk the very same path and suffer the exact same fate as my Dad. And if such does come to pass, I promise not to view it as being a punishment, but rather a well-deserved dose of appropriate parity.

(Continued)

Since then, there are times when I see in my sons' eyes and hear in their words what my Dad must have detected in mine. Each time I feel they're not really paying attention to what I'm asking, explaining, or just simply trying to say serves as a constant reminder of that regretful day.

I've learned the hard way that merely paying attention costs nothing, whereas not doing so can cost you more than you can ever pray to repay. My only comfort is in believing that my Dad forgave me back then, as I understandably and unconditionally forgive my sons now.

I don't know which is harder, convincing myself to forgive myself or waiting for that blessed day when I can finally hear my Dad say how he too understood and yes, had forgiven me as well.

I don't blame you for thinking poorly of me, but believe me,
no matter how bad you see me to be, it doesn't even
begin to compare to how I see myself to not
have been ... and much too often.

I Miss This No More

One of the first things I missed about my Dad was his quick-witted humor and quiet contagious laughter. At first, with no longer hearing this, it really bothered me, but surprisingly enough, I miss this no more.

I can say this only because each and every time I now laugh, I can both hear and feel my Dad laughing not just with me but through me.

This is why when I laugh, I smile so very much. It's not because of what I'm laughing at ... but rather whom I'm laughing with!

September 22, 2000
Alexandria, LA
For this, I am forever grateful, as well as the fact that I'll be
home for my birthday ... the first time in three years!

Loneliness and grief are constant menacing bedfellows for those who must forever sleep without their love one.

Anchorage, AK
As much as I don't want to think of what this is like,
it hurts me even more to know my Mom must
face this sad fact each and every night.

Though it's said that "misery loves company," I can tell you that it not only makes for a truly poor traveling companion, it dims what little light lies ahead.

Houston, TX ~ Airport

My Dad's passing has caused me to rethink the untold number of things I would give anything to say or do over.

Just think of how much different life would be if the good Lord allowed us to feel that same sense of regret well before our actions turned into just that.

Regret, like loss and sorrow, are all unavoidable and daily
factors of life brought on by the loss of a love one.

If you ever find yourself to be more concerned about how poorly what you did or said made you look, rather than how bad you made another feel, just be mindful that your lack of compassion has made you wrong twice over.

For this to really matter, one must truly to care how others
feel about them; otherwise nothing else will ever matter.

Without exception, my Dad had a way of making things seem to be so much better than they could ever really be.

December 25, 2000
We relived good old times we had with Dad and of the many Christmases past.
With tear-filled eyes we both wished him a very Merry Christmas.

It's only now that I'm beginning to truly appreciate the full and complete depth of my Dad's inner wisdom and his quiet, insightful nature. I can only pray my sons will come to see and think of me even half as much as I do of him.

To be more like my Dad, I'll have to change both my way of thinking but also better conform to his way of living.

January 1, 2001
Happy New Year, Dad!

Contentment Delayed

A truly contented heart takes temporary comfort not only from being at peace with itself but by drawing strength and inspiration from its instinctive ability to motivate others to genuinely feel and be at peace with themselves as well.

Final contentment will ultimately come the day we're forever reunited with our departed love ones where together we'll patiently await all those yet to come.

Though unintended, by comforting others we'll get back
much more than we can ever dream to receive.

I'm Begging

There are so many times I feel like my Dad is walking right beside me, or maybe even just a few steps ahead.

And each time I try to catch up with him, reality sets in, and I'm sadly disappointed instead.

Dear God, with all the good You know that I'm trying to do, would it help any if I were to beg for me to spend just a few precious seconds with my Dad?

Denver, CO ~ Airport
If so, then please consider this
as my heartfelt plea!

How does one ever come to terms with continually feeling the loss of what they prayed never to lose?

Ontario, CA ~ Airport
Clearly, this is but one more of the many costs that
death forever imposes on our aching hearts.

Sometimes if you say even one wrong, misspoken word, albeit unintentionally, you're likely to have said entirely too much.

San Antonio, TX
I suggest if you ever find yourself having to think of something
sympathetic to say, you just keep quiet and listen while
your heart and soul prevent you from only fulfilling
the "pathetic" part of what you're seeking.

Don't Wait Until

Whatever it takes, don't wait until after a love one has passed to try and tell them how much they meant to you, or how much you still dearly love them. Such futile attempts provide only a temporary reprieve and don't really help when it comes time to grieve.

So, you need to seize every possible occasion to show just how much you love another while there's still some time left to do so. Believe me, this'll make their absence much easier to mourn, and even their passing considerably less painful to endure. **Years**

Again, please don't wait until it becomes too late, for attempting to reach out to a lost love one's lingering spirit will only dishearten the both of you.

Seeing the sparkle in their eyes and sensing the change in their entire being when hearing such thoughtful and loving words coming not just from your lips but from deep down within your soul is simply irreplaceable. Such tender and caring moments will continue on to soothe both hearts for all of eternity.

April 14, 2001
Never have three years passed so slowly, yet so swiftly.
Time has proven itself to not be something we
need to live by, but to live for.

Questions and Answers

If you find yourself having a problem answering heartfelt questions of faith, you should neither fear your uncertainty nor ever take your sense of indecision as a sign of doubt.

Hidden well beneath the wavering of one's devotion lie more telling questions needing to be answered than just simply one's faith.

Issues left unresolved, following the passing of a love one, give birth to a host of unanswerable questions with the strength of our faith being but only one of many.

Lafayette, LA
So, what questions might you have, or
answers you may be seeking?

Do You Believe ... or Not?

For those who tend to believe that there is no God, I have but one question. I'd like to ask them to simply think back to the last time they were confronted with a truly critical situation. You know; the kind that's well beyond one's ability to control all alone, and with absolutely no one else around to help.

If they can assuredly declare that they've never prayed for the Almighty's help, nor did the thought of ever doing so cross their mind, then sadly, they neither know nor accept that they have a God.

Then, there are the rest of us who gladly admit to seeking His help and divine intervention, on any number of occasions. And during trying times when we are unable to do so for ourselves, what we hear in the dead of the night is our spirit speaking to God on our behalf.

It is our faith that encourages us to listen to those quiet sounds coming deep down from within, for in our hearts we know they're precious messages coming directly from Him.

St. Louis, MO
Too bad, and too often, as it was with me, it takes
an unimaginable loss to finally bring us
around to truly believing.

More Thoughts on Tears

Once again, I see how the taste of but a single tear becomes painfully bitter following the passing of one so dear. Then, as they begin to gather and stream down our face, at a slow but ever-increasing pace, we sadly and hopelessly wipe them away, though all the while knowing their unseen trails are there to forever stay.

Yet, much like the air we breathe, tears give us a badly needed, albeit brief, reprieve. But, unlike the limited breaths we'll take in, our unrelenting tears will not soon end, for our loss hurts in ways that simply can't be explained, as the pain continues to creep back in, upsetting our hearts again ... and yet again.

Houston, TX ~ Airport
Though you can cry along with another, it helps so much
more if you also comfort them while they weep.

We must be especially careful when expressing our sympathies, no matter how sincere we think we are, for it's one of a few very select and uniquely individual emotional exchanges where there are no second chances a getting it right; that's even if there is such a way.

This came to me after paying my respects to a truly good friend. Earlier, I overheard another co-worker struggling to express what I knew to be his true sense of sorrow. Then, in talking to him later, I could tell how he truly wished he had just remained quiet instead ... which he probably should have.

A Few More Words on Sympathy

Most of us have been programmed from our early youth to respond with words of sympathy to anyone who has lost a love one. However, the one thing we're seldom taught is that to offer up such concern without expressing true sincerity are words better left unsaid, for there are times when being thoughtfully quiet more than speaks for itself.

With a somewhat clearer but nonetheless troubled mind, I now see where those who said the very least often expressed the most. They chose to say nothing at a time when there was nothing to be said. Instead, they remained silent, allowing our hearts to talk in a way that mere words alone were never meant to convey.

This is sort of an expanded view of my previous entry, for there are times when I too was sorry for saying something that was better left unsaid.

We don't necessarily get wiser as we age, we just tend to get a lot better at avoiding what's likely to turn into a regretful act before it becomes one.

August 2001
Honolulu, Hawaii ~ Heading to Pearl Harbor
I can only pray that what we've learned from this tragedy makes us all the wiser.

If quietly hugging or even just tenderly touching someone who's truly grieving doesn't move your heart as much as it does theirs, then likely yours hasn't been touched deep enough, at least not yet.

But one day it will be, and when you finally feel that tenderest of touches, don't just embrace it, passionately return it; for it'll do the both of you a world of good.

August 2001
Pearl Harbor, Hawaii ~ National Memorial
This is a very emotional place, even if you're nothing but a mere visitor.

Emotions

As I stated in my first, opening quote, I believe everyone experiences grief, regret, and remorse as instant consequences following the loss of a love one. Yet, dealing with these emotions becomes a lifelong learn-as-you-go experience, for which there are no rules or instructions to follow.

Every emotion has its own unique effect on us. Some seek to calm and console, while others work like a relentless tag-team, taking turns disrupting your every effort to gather even the simplest of thoughts.

There are some emotions that never sleep or rest. Each time you lay your head down they quickly return, causing your pillow to become as dispassionate as a cold, wet slab of stone.

Conflicting emotions hold your dreams hostage by interrupting what little peace or solitude you quietly pray for. They don't wait for you to peacefully arise; instead they abruptly awaken you, setting the pace for that very day, as well as all those to follow.

Believe me, rehashing the many things you would now do differently won't help to lessen your pain, nor will repenting such misdirected actions serve to bring your lost love ones back again.

So, in order to get through till tomorrow we must first cope with today by learning to accept what we can't forget, all the while praying for God's help along the way.

August 2001
Pearl Harbor, Hawaii ~ National Memorial
This was inspired by the expressions I see on many
of the faces of those I'm standing with.

I pray there'll never, ever be any differences between us, as a people, so important, threatening, or immediate that will warrant mankind doing what was done on this very spot ... ever again!

August 2001
Pearl Harbor, Hawaii ~ National Memorial
May the souls of these brave soldiers who now lie resting beneath our feet forever
protect those to follow by serving as a prime example of what can happen
when we senselessly compete to the point of mutual defeat.

The unforgivable tragedies that occurred on this hallowed ground will forever stand as one of the most shameful examples of what people have done to others not because they must, but rather ... just simply because they can.

August 2001
Pearl Harbor, Hawaii ~ National Memorial
I can only thank God that my
Dad wasn't here.

During times of despair consoling words fail to repair a broken heart that's been torn apart by endless grief to which there's little to no lasting or meaningful relief.

And though the mere passage of time has somewhat eased my mind, I'm just now beginning to feel a bit of long-term reprieve, for in my heart I've finally come to believe that a love one's passing is a life everlasting.

August 2001
Pearl Harbor, Hawaii ~ National Memorial
Trying to sense if attending love ones are
feeling the same sense of regret as do
I when I visit with my Dad.

Only Halfway

Losing my Dad put a hole halfway through my heart. I can say halfway only because I still have my Mom.

On that inevitable day when God takes her away, my heart will hurt like only once before, but this time it'll be all the more. For with the both of them gone, I'll be left to forever mourn with having neither around to rely upon.

Naturally, I'll miss my Mom; yet in another odd sort of way, there's some hidden comfort I can draw from her passing, for she'll finally be back to where she truly wants to be ... by my Dad's side for all of eternity.

August 2001
Oahu, Hawaii
As you'll eventually see, the prophecy of this entry sadly came true,
which ultimately caused me to pause all this ... albeit temporarily.

A Close Encounter

While leaving a gift shop, I stepped back to allow this little kid to pass. In doing so I bumped into a young lady standing behind me. As I began to apologize, she smiled and said, "Oh, you're okay. I work here. If I can be of any assistance to either of y'all, please don't hesitate to ask."

At first, I didn't think much of this as I took her to be referring to me and the child who had just entered the store. Yet, by the time I apologized my little friend was already gone. Then, with me being all alone, I looked around to see if maybe I was possibly blocking someone else from leaving or coming in. Yet, again, there was nobody but me and the store clerk. As she crossed in front of me she said, "Here, let me. I'll get the door for y'all."

When I went to thank her, I can only assume with my not seeing anyone else near me, the look on my face must have confused her. What she said next made this entire trip all the more worthwhile, "Oh, I'm so sorry, I thought y'all were together. Please enjoy yourselves and come back."

Still with no one around me, all I could think to say was, "You have no idea how good you've made my day, and yes, I assure you ... we'll both be back!"

August 2001
Kauai, Hawaii
She had to have seen the one person I so long to see.

The only thing that warms my heart more than memories of my Dad's embrace is having faith that come one day I will embrace him again.

August 2001
Waikiki, Hawaii
Now that's really something to look forward to.

Unlike your restless spirit, your heart allows you to forget some things that are too painful to remember. However, such lapses in memory don't last forever, for simply ignoring such pain doesn't ever make it go away.

So, don't confuse failing to recall something with your heart's need to just set it aside until you're ready to deal with it.

August 16, 2001
I'll be heading home later today. ☹

Reason Enough

Until my Dad's passing, I never fully realized the true power that sorrow and grief would have over me.

Prior to this, I always thought of death in simple terms of how it affected me in the here and now. Seldom did its lingering effects continue much beyond the setting of that day's sun.

Please believe that this was not because I'm cold or in any way, dispassionate; it's just that my heart had not yet been truly tested.

Now, every time sorrow and grief try to overtake me, I turn to my Dad and silently ask him what would he do?

Quite frequently, many of his replies turn out to be one of those "aha" moments. Then, sometimes instead of just giving me the answers I seek, he poses an insightful question or two for me to consider.

Earlier today when my heart truly needed some long overdue relief, I did as I often do; I visited with my Dad. As always, he managed to soothe and fill my emotional void, but this time with the most insightful question he's yet to utter, "Because I know you love me just as much as I love you, both then and now, shouldn't this be reason enough for you to no longer grieve?"

Westlawn Cemetery
Though he knew I really wanted and needed to hear that,
if only what he had suggested were that simple.

Tears ... Yet Again

Tears are as secretive as they are revealing. While they sometimes quietly announce the yet to be spoken truth, they often expose even more sorrowfully hidden, silent lies.

It's not without reason that God chose to have tears come from our eyes, for are they not the windows to our heart and soul?

And if you can quickly or easily wipe them away, then clearly, they weren't meant to stay; but it's all those whose traces forever remain behind that truly reveal so much more of what was really on our mind.

Fort Worth, TX
I'm just missing my Dad and worrying constantly
about my son who's now in Kuwait.

Please excuse the interruption...

A short while ago the world learned of multiple horrific tragedies that occurred in New York City, Washington, DC, and Pennsylvania. Apparently, two commercial airliners crashed into both World Trade Centers, a third into the Pentagon, and a fourth went down in a desolate field somewhere in Pennsylvania. My heart aches to say this, but all were fully occupied with US-based air crews and a variety of passengers.

Like so many others, I'm left to watch the devastation from afar. With what I see and sense, I fear the eventual death toll will grow and serve to compound the impact of this disaster. If what's being reported turns out to be true, not only will our faith be tested, but our view of life, love, and liberty is destined to forever change.

As the day progressed, and we learned more of what had actually happened, my mind raced like only once before. Considering the unbelievable degree of carnage and destruction, I pray we learn how this could possibly have taken place. Yet, regardless of the politically correct explanations we'll eventually be given, why this occurred is the one question that will likely never be satisfied, for regardless of the reason it will forever be remorsefully unacceptable.

My anguish and sorrow were clearly focused on the victims, both those found and yet to be uncovered, as well as their many surviving love ones. However, as the day grew old, the collective pain and concern for these innocent, ill-fated souls spread across all lands. Then, as recovery floodlights cast a gloomy glow over the debris, a wave of vengeance and harsh retaliation slowly began to numb our otherwise forgiving hearts. Later, when I had time to review the scraps of paper I had scribbled my initial thoughts and notes upon, I also realized how anger, fear, and revenge were struggling to override my better judgment and emotions.

Even as darkness silently fell upon the entombing rubble, the relentless first responders took this as added motivation to neither give up nor give in. Countless times they put their own lives on the line so others could live, or simply to return the yet to be counted lost souls to their grieving love ones.

(Continued)

News reports and individual accounts were filled with endless acts of fellow coworkers' true heroism, along with miraculous stories of personal fortitude. Once I had time to somewhat take in all that had occurred, my thoughts became redirected to what might still be yet to come.

This is when my thoughts became focused on my youngest son and these "Acts of Terror," as they're being called, quickly became personal. With him being in the military, I began to fear how we would retaliate, how soon, and to what degree? My worries for those yet trapped slowly but painstakingly increased my fears for what my son might also be called upon to face.

Clearly, nowhere on God's green earth are things as good or morally right as they should be. Nonetheless, when we reflect back upon what these collective tragedies will have proven to now be possible, they will serve as the one catalyst that forever changed our lives. All things will simply not be as they once were or could have possibly ever been.

September 11, 2001
Kansas City, KS
I'm praying that I'm not just wrong ... but terribly wrong!

As a point of information...

This is the first time since my Dad's passing that something has moved me so emotionally that I am driven to reenergize my pen, albeit from a totally different perspective. Once again, I take refuge and comfort in capturing all my heart finds too painful to say.

As I look into the eyes of the survivors and first responders, I see that same sense of loss I remember feeling when I lost my Dad. Now don't take this wrong, for in no way am I attempting to compare my loss to what these poor souls are now facing, or even have yet to learn. All I'm saying is that my loss gives me more than enough reason and empathy to hurt for theirs.

Well, before the dust had even begun to settle, I began jotting down my thoughts, feelings, and emotions before they escaped me. As it turned out, right then and there another book was born ... Today Be Damned!

Many of my friends who've read those writings have suggested that because of how similarly and passionately they too speak of love and loss, as well as grief and regret, I should insert a few excerpts for you to consider. Many have gone on to tell me that simply because these writings also have my Dad's fingerprints all over them, they rightfully belong together.

So, I pray our collective words manage to bestow some sense of justice and respectful remembrance to the victims of 09/11. I also hope to convey some thoughtful consolation to each of their heartbroken survivors.

Today Be Damned!

I can think of only one other time that has caused me to view a day that must be remembered as having the same lasting significance as one that should never be forgotten; then along came today.

Why must we always learn the hard way just how truly vulnerable we are, and then to be taught such a brutal, deadly lesson from some cold-blooded, cowardly, veiled assassins from afar?

With our world forever changed, and countless lives rearranged, we're left to question if the worst has yet to come? For only God truly knows just how many poor souls lie buried beneath the tons of rubble below a dust-filled setting sun.

So, tonight I will pray like only once before, that this was but a bad dream and nothing more.

Then, since the true reality of this tragedy will take countless years for us to fully comprehend, all I can think to say until that day is "Today Be Damned!"

September 11, 2001
Kansas City, KS
Unlike Between the Beats, this title came about immediately
and quite naturally, for I feel today will prove to be a day
amongst all others that is truly ... To Be Damned!

Only a heart that already knows the hurt brought on by the loss of a love one can truly hear and feel the otherwise indescribable torment deeply concealed in another's quiet sigh of total despair.

September 11, 2001
Kansas City, KS
Listening to a young lady try to explain the sheer pain of her yet uncertain loss
made the horrific events of today hurt all the more. Her inability
to speak caused me to recall when I too couldn't find the
words that would explain the true depth of such pain.

Every moment of love you leave behind and fail to share will one day come to feel like a lifetime of love lost forever.

September 11, 2001
Kansas City, KS
A thought that will one day cross the minds of today's
survivors as it did mine any number of times.

First Today ... Then Tomorrow

Why is it not until our lives are all but shattered, and the familiar ground upon which we once stood no longer sure, do we only then begin to comprehend how everything we naïvely took for granted can so easily and completely get stripped away?

We stood speechless and powerless, and watched in awe, as the Twin Towers crumbled, and our freedoms tumbled, with no way of stopping the apocalypse we saw.

Due to the events of today we will never be the same; for as of today we are no longer the same. We have been forever changed by a faction of people we knew not, led by a deeply demented, spineless bastard that cares not, who pulled off a feat so damn horrendous that not even he could have envisioned the totality of its outcome.

As much as I am compelled to concern myself with the unknown horrors of tomorrow, the reality of such a senseless tragedy engulfs my troubled mind and fills my worried heart with unbearable sorrow. How do I grieve when I know not yet the depth of how much there'll be to mourn? With that in mind, how can we ever begin to look forward to another tomorrow, knowing that just yesterday, I was truly looking forward to today?

Because there've been so few tragedies, thankfully, to this extent, I predict this particular event will rise above all others. Everyone affected, either directly or simply through observation, will hereafter better appreciate the true value and importance of all those they hold near and dear. I, myself, now see where every single moment spent with love ones and close friends is so much more precious than all the uncertain tomorrows yet to come.

So, before another sun can rise we must first, somehow, get through what remains of today. And only then will we be able to sadly look back at what will have become the senseless, indescribable, and inescapable tragedy of yesterday.

September 11, 2001
Kansas City, KS
God, please bless all the souls that were dreadfully lost today,
and give others both the strength and compassion
to aid and comfort their surviving love ones.

A tragic loss changes many things, but nothing more quickly, permanently, and completely than what we once thought to be important.

September 11, 2001
Kansas City, KS
Many of the survivor's comments reminds me losing my Dad,
and of everything they have yet to face.

Journeys

Though most journeys have a starting point, there's no guarantee you'll return to where you first began. Yet, the voyage of a lost love one is a journey where their survivors want only to go but one way ... up to a loving God, where they pray they will forever stay.

Most excursions bring us back to where we started. Then, there are others that have no particular destination in mind and are taken for utterly unknown reasons with no regard to place or time.

Yet, the longest voyage we'll ever travel begins when all other journeys come to their end. For this one will take everyone up to and through the doorstep of eternity, where till the furthest reaches of time they'll forever spend.

September 11, 2001
Kansas City, KS
With all flights canceled and having a rental car, I'll soon be leaving to drop off fellow
travelers throughout TX and LA in an attempt to get everyone back home.

When I first began to write, I did so in trying to escape from reality.

I now find myself concocting reasons to escape from reality just so I can go off and find some quiet time to write.

September 12, 2001
Well, we're somewhere on the road between Kansas City and home.
Yesterday is but another example of how we should never,
take our love ones for granted ... ever again!

If you think true soul mates are hard to find, wait till you lose one! As such, I worry about what I feel to be quietly lurking behind my Mom's empty smiles.

I now see where hers are much the same as the 09/11 survivors, which is why I earnestly pray that they both, somehow and someway, can find some peace ... someday.

<table>
<tr><td>

An introduction of what's to follow...

Well, here I am, yet once again, far away from home and on the third out of my last four birthdays. However, this one would turn out drastically different.

Being the ever-resourceful person, my Dad has always been, he stepped up to save the day. Let there be no doubt that what happened today neither would nor could have possibly ever occurred if it weren't for his thoughtful, insightful, and creative intervention.

As you're about to read, future birthdays can and will never possibly be more memorable than how this one turned out.

I hope you enjoy reading this as much as I did recalling it.
</td></tr>
</table>

My Fiftieth Birthday

Long before the tragedy of September 11, 2001, I made arrangements to attend a convention in Miami, Florida. While there, I was hoping to celebrate my fiftieth birthday; however, such would not be the case. Pat's fear of flying following the tragic events of 09/11 changed all that. My luck being what it is, I once again ended up all alone and yes, far, far from home. Yet, this time it wasn't on just any old birthday; it was my one and only fiftieth!

With Pat not there to share in my impending midlife crisis, I had no real desire to rejoice or even celebrate. To keep anyone from finding out what was soon to pass, I told no one. In fact, with all the partying going on, I offered to go to the airport and escort the last few convention attendees to the hotel. By this time, I knew my one and only fiftieth birthday celebration wasn't going to be anything like I had hoped it might.

So, quietly, my nearly fifty-year-old butt boarded the bus to the airport. At 11:40 PM I found myself sitting at the end of absolutely the longest, loneliest, and most deserted airport concourse I've ever been in. Not another person was in sight, except for an elderly black gentleman working a little further down from where I disappointedly sat.

Having time to do little more than mope over my failed monumental birthday bash, I sulked and consoled myself. I repeatedly thought, why me ... why always me? I mean, isn't one's fiftieth birthday more special than all the rest? Maybe, just maybe, if I manage to make it to my sixtieth it'll be better. I guess I'll just have to wait and see.

(Continued)

When I looked up, there stood that elderly gentleman gazing directly at me, with a rather perplexed look upon his face. Not knowing what to say, I asked him, "So, how's your day going?" He paused, smiled, and while laughing he replied, "Looks like yours ain't goin' much bett'a than mine." Before I knew it, I had blurted out, "You have absolutely no idea and wouldn't believe me, even if I told you!" He laughed again and said, "Hell ... try me!"

We both had a really good laugh when I explained how I ended up there and of my failed fiftieth birthday ball. Following a brief discussion of how his workday was going, I asked him, "Is there anywhere I might get me a beer?" He looked at his watch, grinned, and quickly replied, "Nope, not you, but I know where I can go git us some!"

The only thing quicker than the twenty bucks I slipped to him was his coming back with two rather large cups of the coldest, absolutely best-tasting beer I've ever had. In an impromptu instant, my once-in-a-lifetime birthday would not be going uncelebrated, and certainly not alone.

As my newfound friend took his first sip, he snuck behind one of those small portable sales carts with a look in his eyes that I should follow, so I did. After a few more sips, and some small talk, he set his cup down, dug into his pocket, and returned the twenty dollars I had given him. Bearing the kind of smile that only comes with age, he remarked, "I bet ya' thought I forgot about your change. This one's on me ... Happy Birthday!" To stop my insistence that he keep the money, he took one last swallow and wished me a very happy birthday as he walked away.

Before I took my final sip, I called out to get his attention, raised my cup, and gave him a departing toast. I tried to tell him that he'd never know just how much I truly appreciated what he did. He stopped, gave me one final grin with a thumbs-up, and uttered, "Oh, yes I do!"

It was at that very moment when I realized we were not alone, for my Dad had to have orchestrated this entire, once in my lifetime happening.

As my newfound friend worked his way down the concourse, I could feel my Dad standing right next to me, laughing and celebrating with every word and sip. Considering how I thought this evening would end, it could not have turned out any better. You've got to admit ... my Dad really outdid himself today. What a birthday!

(Continued)

A few minutes later, the people I had been waiting for finally arrived. On our way to get their luggage, I saw my drinking buddy a few feet down another corridor, still hard at work. So, I stopped the group and asked them to wait a minute while I walked over to him. When he shook my hand, I pressed that same twenty dollars firmly into his and told him that on his next birthday he needed to go have a beer; this time it's on me. He winked, shook my hand again, and happily smiled while promising he would.

With my group looking on, their curiosity had gotten the best of them. Upon my return, it was almost as if a few of them had rehearsed it when they asked in unison, "What the hell was that all about? Who's he?" I stopped and hollered back to my new friend, "Hey! They want to know who you are?" He smiled with that same old pleasant grin and replied, "Just tell 'em I'm da' Birthday Man!"

I'm sorry for repeating myself, but although this day surely didn't turn out anything like it started, or even how I had hoped it would, it absolutely and positively could not have ended any better!

Though it was truly a one-of-a-kind birthday, you've got to admit ... I've got a one-of-a-kind Dad!

September 22, 2001
Miami, FL ~ Airport
I pray someone makes my new friend's next birthday as special as he made mine, and he has a really cold beer on me. Believe me, I truly thank ... da' Birthday Man!

They

I'm sure there are those who truly believe they've experienced similar pain and anguish as another, or even suffered the same despair as did they. However, I pray they not make the horrid mistake of saying that they know just how the other must feel, for they can't, and they never will.

Similar circumstances often cause us to view our situation to be closely aligned with another. It's kind of like stepping into someone else's footprint. Yes, you can, but not until they step out of it, and the impression you leave behind will never be the same as theirs.

So, please, always be mindful that just like your paths differed, so will what it takes to get you to where they are.

September 23, 2001
South Beach, FL
Time changes absolutely everything for everyone ... forever.

Now ... Tears and Laughter

Leave it up to the Almighty to bestow upon us two vastly differing and conflicting emotions. What better way is there to cleanse our souls and free our hearts than with tears and laughter?

When we either cry or laugh, we feel an immediate release of not only what's hiding just below the surface, but also that which is deeply buried within.

Sometimes we uncontrollably shed tears when we laugh, which is a good thing. Then, when we hurt so badly that absolutely nothing else matters, we shed tears once again. This time they don't just cover up the pain, but rather soothe what little of our aching heart still remains.

The more I thought about this, the more I realized that one's life will be neither complete nor fulfilled if they're never moved to both cry and laugh.

Though the emotions that torment our hearts the most usually get buried deeply in the recesses of our mind, the good Lord knowing they must eventually be released and allows us to do so, we pray, at only the right place and time.

December 25, 2001
Tonight, my Mom and I shared stories that brought on tears
of joy and pain, yet once again. Merry Christmas, Dad.

It's simply a reality that come one day we're all going to lose a love one, that's if they don't lose us first. And I know you've already heard this, but should we not then live each and every day like there may be no tomorrow?

So, might I suggest you seriously reconsider your plans for this evening. Yet, if for some reason you don't have any, or a love one is not included, please put this down and do nothing else until you go make some ... with them!

Omaha, NE
I fear the many tomorrows I've yet to experience will never come even close to but one
of the yesterdays I failed to share with my Dad. This is why I try to spend as much
time with my love ones as I can; so, they won't experience my many regrets.

Watch What You Ask For

Who better to review my words and intentions than the one person that knows me better than anyone else, the love of my life, my lovely wife, Pat. Recently, after reading my first draft, I asked her if anything needed correcting, and what were her thoughts on what I tried to say. The pause that followed had me figuring that she was either trying to find the right words to applaud my efforts or figure out a way to say something I might otherwise not wish to hear. As it turned out, it was quite a bit of both.

She began by reading aloud the comment at the bottom of my previous entry. Then, after a long and bothersome pause, what she said next was as disturbing as it was oddly reassuring. She continued with "I know you. I know your heart. I know how much you miss your Dad and now, your Mom ... I miss both of mine too. Yet, it bothers me to think that with all we have, with two wonderful children and all of our grandchildren, and spending almost our entire lives together, I'm sorry, but all of that should rank right up there with anything and anyone else. However, your words repeatedly indicate that your life is all but meaningless since your Dad's passing. I know you're down, too often, too much, and for far too long. But I also see the joy in your eyes when you're with our sons and grandkids, or when you find just the right words to say what I can only wish I could. Your life has so much more meaning than you give yourself credit for. It hurts me to see you beat yourself down faster and further than I can ever hope to lift you. Believe me, we all love you more than you'll ever know!"

Boy ... I guess I'd better be more careful about what I ask for! Her reply wasn't anything like what I expected, but it was exactly what I needed: the unadulterated truth and all that that encompassed. Though what she said makes me regret writing some of what you've already read, as well as what you've yet to read, it nonetheless represents my feelings, during those mournful times. Since I tend to not edit my standing words if doing so would alter their initial intent, I made a rare but well-warranted exception. I went back and edited my previous comment to further clarify all that I first meant to say. However, everything else will remain as written, for the truth is what it is just as my thoughts are what they are. Believe me, I mean no harm.

(Continued)

Now, to my dear Pat, and anyone else who knows me well enough to have also detected what she so caringly shared ... I truly apologize. It's important for all of you to know that it was never and will never be my intention to solely draw attention to my pain alone. Rather, I'm seeking to lessen the emotional load for those who find comfort in knowing that there are others whose heart hurts much the same as does theirs.

To everyone else, if, at times, my words seem too dark and are riddled with phrasing that denotes inescapable pain, all you need to understand is that each passage came directly from my rambling thoughts and notes, for which I alone am the only one to blame.

When the light in my life seems to grow dim, I should take comfort in the fact that, at least, there's still some light. And because my previous comment so rightfully bothered Pat, editing it came about as naturally as did the words that helped to make it much more complete.

A heartfelt and noteworthy observation...

Though Pat had already read much of what I'd previously written and somewhat voiced similar observations as to the overall, let's just say, messages conveyed in many of my writings, never did she ever express herself so emotionally or succinctly.

Her assessment really and truly hit home causing me to pause until I could figure out what I was to do. The slight edit came easy as my previous comment clearly needed to be clarified. Then, a thought hit me that really set me back; was this a sign that it was time for me to simply stop writing and temporarily set this book aside. It didn't take but a few seconds for me to know that I could do neither.

But I did go back and review all my writings only to see that if I edited every entry that fit into Pat's evaluation, this book would get really short, very quickly. As I've already tried to explain, editing, rephrasing, or even toning down some of my writings would be to admit that I didn't fully believe in what I first wrote, and that's absolutely not the case. I feel that if you're not willing to defend or stand behind what you've written, it's time to lay your pen down and go find something else to do! So, editing more than just that one comment was out of the question. Besides, if it's taken me all these years to get to this point, I don't believe I have all that much time remaining to do that much editing.

Or just stop writing and set this book aside ... I don't think so! With what I've referred to as being "my words," when, in fact, they are ongoing communications with my Dad and now my Mom, you've got to know I'm not going to do anything that might possibly jeopardize that collaboration. Just like some people knit, read, exercise, travel, or do whatever they do to please the desires of their heart, writing is one of the things I pray I can continue until either I stop hearing from the both of them or it becomes time for me to join them.

So, I figured I'd just continue doing what I had been doing. And I'm sorry if you view me to be wrong, but as I believe and will say later, yet again, it's okay to be wrong if it's for all the right reasons!

Hummmmm

With life and this world often being in such serious and compelling conflict, I can see where it's easy for some to question how much worse Hell can really be.

This both scares and bothers me, but so does the breaking down of the basic family unit. Too many fathers are willing to abandon their children. Terrorism is all but unrestrained. Devious and dishonest politicians abound, and economic turmoil is wreaking havoc upon practically every working soul.

Now don't take me too literally, but I believe it's truly a sad state of affairs if life's current dilemmas lure some into perceiving death as just another alternative, even if going to Hell appears to be their unavoidable fate.

Cleveland, OH ~ Airport
And yes, although some of my writings may indicate I sometimes feel this way, please don't worry ... I'll be okay.

Worries

Can anyone please tell me that after losing a love one what's so wrong with wanting to just crawl into bed, assume the fetal position, and before anyone finds you, pull the covers tightly over your head?

I don't know about you, but there are so many times when I feel the need to simply escape all the madness and sadness that surrounds me.

As for those who can't relate to this or believe me to simply be foolish for having such rambling thoughts, I worry. I also pray that come one day they'll cast aside their false sense of pride, for maybe then they'll no longer feel shame when they too are finally willing to admit having done or, at least, remember feeling much the same.

And oh yeah ... sucking your thumb is optional.

Just so you'll know...

I wrote this after hearing an evening newscast about the escalation of fighting in Kuwait. Our youngest son, Corey, is proudly serving in the United States Air Force and has been deployed there ... for far too long.

Dear God, whatever time You spend watching over me, instead, please redirect Your efforts to protecting and taking extra care of my son. As You well know, the love I have for him is no different and is just as strong, pure, and true as is Yours for Your son.

A Lesson Learned

Once again, I'm learning the hard way that the time I've spent and wasted while buried in death's denial would have been much better spent creating lasting memories with my many love ones that remain.

January 12, 2002
Stratosphere Hotel & Casino
Las Vegas, NV
It being my Dad's birthday and the first time I'm back in Vegas since his passing,
I went to the same hotel lobby where I received that life-changing call.
It's just as I remember it, and even still smells the same.
Happy Birthday, Dad!

Should Have Said ... or Done

With the emotions that spurred my previous thought still weighing heavily on my mind, I find myself thinking over all the opportunities I failed to take advantage of.

Sadly, not until we're hovering on the brink of regret are most of us motivated to say or do that which we should have long since said or done.

Avoiding a mistake before it can become one fixes a lot more than just what you should have said or done.

Though our worried souls and spirits can continually converse, we mortals are not so fortunate. On that day when both our hearts and love ones are eternally laid to rest, so will our ability to say and do that which can no longer be said or done.

So, if while reading this you caught yourself nodding in regretful agreement, and you are as guilty of this as am I, then stop reading and go say or do that which you feel you should already have said or done.

With the uncertainty of all the days we've yet to face, allowing an aging or ailing love one to see just how much you truly love them, or to feel your closeness and deep affection, now, today, and not putting it off until tomorrow will help the both of you ... even if tomorrow doesn't come for either of you.

February 9, 2002
If you'll heed my suggestion, the next time you read this not
only will my words have more meaning, so will you!
PS: Happy 28th Anniversary to my love, Pat.

If given the opportunity to go back in time, even though you wouldn't be allowed to change anything, just how far back would you really choose to go?

And if you could, with knowing what all has yet to occur, just how willing would you be to return?

March 14, 2002
Arrived in Rome, Italy
Wandering and wondering in a city like none I've ever seen.

Having my Dad quietly whisper to me in the dead of the night, as I lie in the darkness with but a dim night light, motivates me to do many things, but nothing like before, other than to listen to him intently, simply for the joy of hearing more.

March 2002
Rome, Italy ~ The Vatican & Trevi Fountain
As I walked around in amazement, I felt one of the souls resting within the walls of the Rotunda wishing me well and thanking me for all of my caring thoughts.

When your heart cries with another's, you can't help but shed and share much more than just tears.

March 2002
Rome, Italy ~ Catacombs
When a fellow tourist remarked that she didn't like the dampness down in the Catacombs I asked her, "Well, what else would you expect considering the countless tears that's been shed down here for hundreds of years?"
She just gazed at me and walked away.

Why, when only what's viewed to be important people pass on, is it often said the world has lost an irreplaceable treasure?

This offends me, and more so, the more I hear it.

Though my Dad saw and thought of himself to be a common man, rather, from where I stand, it's been over four years since the world lost a lot more than just another irreplaceable treasure. And I'm sure you feel much the same for the love ones you've lost as well.

March 2002
Pompeii, Italy
I say this, if for no other reason than that I believe every love one should be an irreplaceable treasure to someone.

I've Learned to Listen

I used to listen to friends with somewhat mixed feelings, and a slight bit of skepticism, when they spoke about holding ongoing discussions with their departed love ones.

It's not that I disbelieved them or doubted their sincerity, but the sheer joy they seemed to harvest from these mythical conversations always intrigued me.

I could only figure that they knew something I had not yet come to understand, or even believe; but then I lost my Dad.

Reality has a way of focusing our full attention to where it's both most sorely needed and clearly lacking.

So, before I could utter as much as a tearful word, my heart turned up the volume so his voice could be heard. He reassured me by explaining that he was okay, and the talks I once doubted now take place each and every day.

March 2002
Naples, Italy
This place is simply gorgeous, and it is as moving
as it is inspirational to merely be here.

Each time I hear someone say that there's so little in life to be thankful for, I find myself thinking that they surely wouldn't feel that way had they ever met my Dad.

March 2002
Isle of Capri, Italy
Each time I pass a craftsman working on handmade items,
my Dad and I stop to watch and appreciate what people
can do with the many gifts God has given to them.

The best way to remember and honor departed love ones is to know in your heart that you did so every chance you had while they were still here.

To that point, just think of how you'd feel if your love ones would take the time to do so as well.

March 2002
Amalfi Coast, Italy
If my words do nothing else, I pray they don't just make
you aware of this principle, but that they inspire
you to hereafter practice it as well.

Grief is that quiet thief in the middle of the night that robs us of sleep till morning's first light.

March 2002
Sorrento, Italy
Disturbing thoughts interrupt more than just your thoughts.

You can't stand witness to what has boldly stood the formidable test of time without being deeply moved.

March 2002
We're back in Rome, Italy ~ The Vatican
The Sistine Chapel is clearly illuminated by the perpetual shining light of God.

With as much as I write, too often I feel as if I fail to convey exactly what I meant. Repeatedly, emotions cloud my ability to adequately compile just the right words to properly express my true heartfelt intent.

If after writing something it doesn't speak back to me, I will set it aside until a more meaningful conversation takes place. Only then, and with my Dad's help, will it evolve into something we both feel worth sharing.

So, know that what you've read and what lies ahead are by no means all I've written; it's only that portion which we pray now speaks to you as well.

March 2002
Rome, Italy ~ Vatican Courtyard
Though I'll be heading home later today, I'm taking
so much more than I brought with me.

Whenever you write, especially if it has some length to it, and you don't find something to correct or revise each time you reread it, don't view it as being a finished work; just accept the fact that there's something you're still overlooking.

If I had but a few pennies for every time I've revised something within these covers, I could easily give all the copies of it away. However, I think my Dad really enjoys teasing me by asking, "Not again … what this time?"

March 24, 2002
Rome, Italy ~ Airport
For all the generously bestowed upon us by everyone we've met, I have no words
that can come even close to thanking them for their sheer kindness, nor can I
begin to let them know just how lucky they are to be living where they are.

False Hopes

Considering the life I sometimes led as a youngster, I fear God may, and justifiably so, have other plans for me when it comes to reuniting with my Dad, or for that matter, any other deceased love ones. Rightfully, there's a price we must be willing to pay for our ill-gotten deeds; even if its long after it should have been collected.

With this on my mind, the term "false hopes" kept returning. So, after about the third or fourth time, I took that as a sign and my thoughts began to wander in a direction I would have preferred they not go. Then, the more I pondered over my eventual eternal fate, my worries were being replaced by a calming sense of reassurance that could only have come from my slow yet ever-growing beliefs and faith.

This time it didn't feel like this message was coming from my Dad, but something assured me that God would not have set me in the direction He has, and I've long since traveled, only to tease me with false hopes.

Airborne on a flight heading home from Rome
What religious teachings I've had tell me that the good Lord never
teases His followers; instead, He chooses to teach them.
And though it's personally taken me too long to
get to where I am … I've come pretty far.

Forget Something?

Recently, I was upset with myself for not being able to recall something I truly should have. As the next anniversary of my Dad's passing approaches, I couldn't remember if it was three years, or could it possibly already be as many as four?

Then, with the countless, useless, mundane facts I can immediately recall, I thought surely this is one thing I absolutely should remember quicker than any other.

That's when my spirit softly whispered, "Does it really matter if it's been three years, or maybe four, if in your heart it feels like it's been forever and even more?"

Westlawn Cemetery
Though I've read the dated inscribed upon my Dad's tomb
countless times, it always feels like it's the very first.

The Dark Side

Depression nibbles away at its victims one piece at a time, by slowly corroding and methodically eroding what little is left of their aching hearts that remains behind.

By avoiding all exchanges of affection, they protect themselves from what they fear the most ... rejection. And with unruly emotions churning just below their unsure surface, they find few reasons to believe that they serve any useful or worthwhile purpose.

Such deeply buried, conflicting thoughts endlessly haunt, and then **Years** tirelessly taunt, these poor troubled souls lost in time. Caught up in their own wake, I pray for God's sake He blesses them in the hereafter with some badly needed and long overdue peace of mind.

April 14, 2002
Westlawn Cemetery
It is so very scary to think that what feels like just
yesterday has already been four years.

Think of how supportive we could be if our spirit would just simply remind us, well before each day ends, if we've failed to tell a love one just how much we truly love them.

April 14, 2002
Westlawn Cemetery
It's no one's fault but our own, certainly not the Almighty's,
if this is something we're already failing to do.

Just as Much ... and All the Same

In the overall scheme of things, after losing a love one, does it matter who or what's to blame, for will not our hearts continue to hurt ... just as much and all the same?

Though there's a difference if we lose a love one at the hands of another, for it gives us someone upon whom we can vent our anger and pain. Yet, regardless of where we place the blame, we'll still be left broken-hearted over our loss ... just as much and all the same.

Houston, TX
I just learned that a really good friend lost his only son to a drunk driver
who had three previous DUIs. As my friend so poignantly put it,
"Would my heart hurt any less had it been only his first?"

Before we can reminisce in the past, or even begin to look forward to the future, we must first learn to not only cope with the present but deal with all that it's likely to impose upon us.

For once a loss has taken control of our heart and every idle thought, the past will forever after become the heartbreaking present.

Houston, TX
Expressing some thoughtful concern for my friend who had just
lost his son, and another whose wife recently passed away,
and how they must now continue on without them.

Temporarily

With my Dad's death temporarily separating us, I can hardly wait till the day when mine finally brings us back together, foronce and forever.

Portland, OR
And no, I didn't misspell "foronce"! Please read on.

A suggested word change...

After writing my above entry it occurred to me that the merging of the two words "for" and "ever" into "forever" has well served the purpose for which this grammatical fusion was clearly intended.

That's when I realized that since the words "for" and "once" draw together the very same emotions and timelines as does "forever," albeit at a different point in time, I felt that they should be merged into one as well

So, I would ask that you reread my above entry to see if you would then agree that to want something as badly as being reunited with a departed love one, even if only but "foronce," is to truly desire the very same thing "forever"?

Fail not to heed the value contained in regret and remorse, for there are few lessons in life that come with such a cost, as well as a clear message and purpose.

Your spirit will challenge you with these emotions not so much to have you repeat or repent, but rather to try and appease your heart's longing desire to both forever forgive and forget.

Omaha, NE ~ Airport
And as life goes on you'll come to see that it doesn't really
matter much which emotion gives rise to the other.

For those times when you find yourself somewhere, anywhere, but for whatever reason your spirit doesn't seem to be with you, then you may very well be somewhere you really ought not to be.

Omaha, NE
With that said, thankfully, I'll be
heading home tomorrow.

An Admonishment of Myself

At first, the loss of my Dad served to strengthen and justify my already uncertain belief that there may be no God; for if there was, why would He take someone so dear to so many, while leaving the likes of me behind?

As someone once said, "There are no atheists in foxholes!" For I too found myself praying to God; not as a last resort, but He was the only one I felt could make right this wrong. Though the answers I sought were not what I received, the sheer comfort I found in quiet, heartfelt prayer caused me to begin questioning much of what I had formerly doubted and tended to disbelieve.

Then, what could I say that might move Him to undo what He had done, if that was even possible? Maybe, if He took me instead, or just as well, my pain would either lessen or somehow go away?

Though I'm no longer opposed to what others tell me I should believe; then, at the same time, my rebellious mind has trouble accepting what my aching, uncertain heart can't yet fully conceive.

So, I hesitate to tell you this, but there's still no bright light at the end of my seemingly endless tunnel. I've chosen to hide nothing, as I no longer feel I have anything left to hide. To tell you that I've been reborn would greatly mislead you. Then, to say that I continue to disbelieve as strongly as I once did would be as inaccurate as it is untrue.

September 22, 2002
Westlawn Cemetery
Well, with me being in such a bad mood, and on my birthday, I figured
I'd go visit with my Dad, as he always makes me feel better.
In spite of my frame of mind, just simply being near him
turned this into truly a much happier day!

Maybe because we had so much to talk about, but yet at times so little to say, is why we now find ourselves in such deep conversations and at some of the oddest times each and every day.

Ontario, CA
Please know that I'm trying to change this with my sons.

What Moves Us

Even the coldest of hearts are so easily stimulated. The familiar sound of a friendly voice or a genuine, caring smile can soothe, heal, and tame the kinds of pain that absolutely no medicine could ever hope to cure.

A tender touch during trying times will quickly revive even the most uncaring of troubled souls. And it takes but three simple notes from a song we'd long since thought forgotten to cause even the quietest of spirits to vocally erupt releasing suppressed fantasies of stardom.

With all of this in mind, why is it that so many people are so quick to become so callous and dispassionate? Maybe if we took the time to look close enough behind their cold steel façade, we'd see a soul searching for the love they had been denied.

Would not the precious time we all waste concealing our feelings and emotions be much better spent sharing the many delights of our hearts instead?

December 25, 2002
I'm often as moved as I am surprised by the words and
thoughts my Dad chooses to pass on through me.
Merry Christmas, Dad, from both Mom and me.

While spending Christmas with Mom, as always, we talked about Dad. At one point, she left the room and came back in with a box containing some of his things, which included an old pair of shoes. At her request, I slipped them on.

Seeing that they fit, she told me to keep them. I then found myself telling her, "I'd be glad to, but just because they fit doesn't mean I'll ever be able to fill them." She smiled and said, "Don't worry ... you already have!"

December 25, 2002
And oh yeah ... thanks for the shoes Dad!

He Tried So Hard

My Dad continues to teach and inspire me, even in his absence. In fact, there's a chance that since his passing, I've actually learned the most. And it's not because my aging has made me more scholarly; it's just taught me to better filter what's really worth learning.

In spite of my youthful stubbornness, my Dad and Mom patiently took the time to show me all the little things that eventually made me into who I am today. Yet, though he's gone, at least in terms of the here and now, he's still somehow passing on all that will ultimately determine who I am yet to be.

One of the more important things he tried to teach me was that just because our heart's ability to forgive is in a constant battle with our ingrained propensity to not forget, it's never too late to do either. This is true even up to the very moment just before we take our last and final breath. I'm sorry to say this, but I'm still struggling to fully accept and abide by this principle, for there are a few things I've done that I wouldn't think to ask my Dad to forgive; though I know he has.

As I pondered over what I've thus far tried to tell you about my Dad, I believe I've inadvertently revealed much more about myself instead. For this, I'm sorry, as it was truly not my intention to do so.

My Dad not only continues to inspire me to conceive such thoughts, but he has instilled in me a deep passion to share my feelings with anyone who's willing to listen to my compulsive, unrestrained ramblings.

I would hope that my words cause those who never knew him to truly wish they had.

Newark, NJ ~ Airport
Trying to live as he has taught me is the only way I can now
show my appreciation and admiration for all that he
did, tried, and continues to do for me.

Too Many Uns

Though an unexpected loss will haunt you forever, questions that go unasked will breed uncertainty that'll plague you unendingly. And issues left unsettled or unresolved, will unfortunately remain unanswered.

January 12, 2003
Cleveland, OH ~ Airport
And under a clear blue sky, I bid
you a Happy Birthday, Dad!

A Poem for the Lonely

Time after time we force ourselves to smile, finding it harder and harder to believe that any of our efforts are still worthwhile.

We wonder how it might feel to never be depressed, with the answer being something we can only but guess.

In our hearts there's always a lingering, empty sort of feeling, robbing us of what little hope there may be of ever finding life's true meaning.

The anguish we feel comes from years of hurt, nurtured by despair, and having such a profound lack of self-worth, we're at a loss to find real meaningful reasons to ever truly care.

Our prayers each night yield little lasting relief to the torment that engulfs a life filled with such indescribable sorrow and heartfelt grief.

It is only we the lonely that know just how hard it is to pretend, with happiness forever being just beyond our reach, and unrelenting sense of loneliness intruding like an unwelcomed ... uninvited friend.

I wish I had something more positive to say,
but that ain't going to happen today!

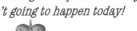

It's not until I too can finally come to see what many of my friends say they see in me will I begin to somewhat see myself a lot more clearly.

Anchorage, AK
And that's only if I'm willing to accept what others
say they see in me as truly being me.

Death provides very unique but clearly unwelcomed opportunities, yet it's absolutely like nothing else I've ever encountered. For once I succumbed to its eternal embrace, I slowly but surely began to understand and accept that it's the one thing that can never be erased.

For now, I can only pray to be reunited with all my departed love ones that Heaven will have gathered together, where we will all become one ... and not just from then on, but forever and ever.

Fort Worth, TX
Sorry, but when my mind gets to wandering
it sometimes goes a bit astray.

I guess it'll take my **5** death to be a clear and final sign that I too have **Years** had enough.

April 14, 2003
Council Bluffs, IA
It's only now that I can look back, in hindsight, at just how much my
Dad quietly suffered, and the personal toll it took on his soul.

Never did I ever think I would one day welcome death as much as I once cherished living.

Memphis, TN ~ Airport
Take it easy; I'm just thinking of what it'll take to one
day see my Dad again, that's praying I do!

I was always somewhat unsure as to what could possibly happen in one's life that would be so tragic to cause them to truly cease looking forward to tomorrow. Then, my Dad passed away, and the answer to this lay hidden no more.

I can still remember that before the first tear dropped from my cheek, I truly cared not if tomorrow ever came and caught myself sincerely praying that it wouldn't.

Los Angeles, CA
A disturbing thought that, at times,
continues to plague me.

I see where it's impossible to ever have a true change of heart without changing more than just your heart.

July 4, 2003
Salt Lake City, UT
The birth of our first grandchild, Gabe, brought tears to my eyes like only
once before, but happily, for a much different reason.

Sleep is but a temporary escape from reality with death being our permanent pillow of rest.

This came to me after speaking to a friend who is trying
to cope with recently losing her Dad.

Death is that unplanned, often unexpected spark that ignites an emotional firestorm burning silently, deep down within.

Then, along comes grief and regret, together serving as an endless supply of kindling, with our love one's absence fanning our flames of depression like a hard, driving wind.

Kansas City, KS
I'm right back to where I was on 09/11, which has
caused me to rethink our mutual losses.

Just when you think you're beginning to accept and move on following a love one's passing, reality quietly, albeit ruthlessly, slips back in.

Totally unassociated things will begin happening that resurrect your loss by awakening memories and emotions you had long since prayed to have been forever laid to rest.

San Antonio, TX
I just pulled over to let a funeral procession go by, and while offering
a silent prayer for their loss, I was sadly reminded of mine.
So, as soon as I get home I'm going to go visit my Dad.

No matter how often sorrow causes one's heart to scream, it's only the bearer of that pain who hears and feels such loud anguishing pleas.

Dallas, TX ~ Airport

Just Like My Dad

While driving home, I stopped at a gas station where I overheard an attendant speaking to another customer. To more than just my delight, he sounded exactly like my Dad. As he started to walk off, I quickly asked him if he could help me with getting back onto the interstate. Hell, I knew exactly where I needed to go; I just wanted to hear him speak some more. Not only did he turn around and come over to me, you could see in his eyes he really enjoyed knowing he was going to be helping me

I was even more pleased to find out that not only did he sound like my Dad, but he also gave me much more information than I had asked for, just like my Dad surely would have.

With every word he spoke, he turned an already good day into an even better one. Since both my sons and Pat had called earlier to wish me a happy birthday, I didn't think today could feasibly get any better, but it did! Unknowingly, this gentleman gave to me a gift no one else possibly could, short of God Himself; a long overdue, one-on-one conversation with my Dad ... even if it was but through another.

Following our welcomed, extended discussion, he asked me, "Where ya' heading?" When I explained that I was going back home, toward New Orleans, he replied, "Boy, I sure wish I was goin' wit' cha'!"

The look on his face to my reply, "You may not know it, but you will be!" was almost as priceless as the intervening discussion I had just had with my Dad. With that, we shook hands, and believe me, it was all I could do to keep from grabbing and hugging him.

No different than if he were sitting right next to me, this heaven-sent messenger was with me for my entire trip home, even if in spirit alone.

Knowing Pat, she'll have something planned for my birthday tonight. However, I hope she won't take this wrong or get offended, but after what happened today, it's really going to have to be something super special to even come close to topping this.

September 22, 2003
Shreveport, LA
Happy, Happy, Happy Birthday to me!

Say What?

Letting your heart speak honestly, openly, and often not only cleanses your soul and relieves your heart but soothes your restless spirit as well.

Since there'll come a time when you too will be silenced forevermore, please don't hold back or even hesitate from saying that which your heart truly longs, yet appropriately, wishes to say.

There are so many things I wished I had said to my Dad, but due to no one's fault but my own, I didn't. And now, trying to break my silence to his ever-lingering spirit is just not the same, and never will be until we're face to face, hopefully, once again.

October 3, 2003
Salt Lake City, UT
This was a rare treat being able to coordinate a business
trip while being with our oldest son on his birthday.
Happy Birthday, Craig!

In the deafening silence of the night those voices you sometimes hear are actually nothing more than your heart, soul, and spirit ever so quietly and passionately whispering to each other.

Albuquerque, NM
And I'm happy to say that quite often I hear my Dad joining in.

Agony Shared

I can no longer bear to view others in pain or stand witness to another's anguish without my heart hurting much the same.

Having come to know the upsetting effects of both loss and grief, my faith gets tested each time I pray for any lasting, long-term relief.

So, when you cry please rest assured that I too am crying just as well, for maybe all the tears we've collectively shed together will someday douse the flames of our mutual living hell.

December 25, 2003
Though I'm really happy to be spending Christmas with Mom,
yet once again, here we are having to struggle while
trying to celebrate it without Dad!

I Remained Silent ... Instead

It's often much easier to remain silent, but at what cost is such refrain? Although I thought to tell my Dad how much I love him so many times, foolishly, I remained silent ... instead.

I still remember the first visit with my Dad, and gently laying my hands upon the cold, engraved stone that now separates us. I prayed like only once before to sense his lingering presence, and even managed to convince myself that I had.

Deep feelings of both guilt and regret moved me to tell him just how much I still love and miss him, but I hung my head, and once again, I could do nothing more than remain silent ... instead.

I've since come to accept that he knows of my feelings, both past and present, and I'm comforted by the fact that he can hear my every thought and whisper.

Because of this, I no longer feel the need to speak during such visits. I now let our hearts and souls do all the talking, and I just simply listen, all the while knowing that it's now okay to remain silent ... instead.

January 12, 2004
Westlawn Cemetery
Another visit with my Dad on yet another of his birthdays.
So, Happy Birthday, Dad ... I love and miss you.

When the voices inside your head seem to be getting louder than the words coming from your lips, it's time to stop and carefully consider not who is it that's doing all the talking, but even more importantly, what is it that's actually being said?

January 12, 2004
Westlawn Cemetery
I'm sorry, Dad, but did you just say something?

Good Advice

You're right; I don't call or visit Mom anywhere near as much as I should, or even could.

And yes, I'm much better at giving others such advice than I am at following that of my own.

Livonia, LA
Just another thoughtful reminder from my Dad, while
on the road, and yes, I promise to go visit
with Mom before going home!

Your Spirit

An old, dear friend, after reading what I had written about my relationship with my spirit, laughingly remarked, "Hell ... I lost touch with my spirit a long time ago. I didn't even think I still had one, but hopefully, we'll get back together."

I explained how you can't lose what was never lost and that one's spirit will forever be their comrade in arms, faithfully rising in their defense when all others seem to have abandoned them. With you and your spirit conjoined forever, the two of you are inseparable.

I also described how our spirits quietly communicate through tender touches, and gentle nudges, in the middle of the night. And when no one else is near, they'll take on what we most fear, by ensuring that all things will turn out just right.

It may come to you as but a cool, refreshing breeze on a calm, hot summer's day, or an encouraging word, softly and quietly whispered by a lost love one, and in a way that only they know how to convey.

Your spirit will soothe your troubled soul and protect all that your heart holds dear. Then, just when you think there's nowhere else to turn, it'll open closed doors, giving you many more through which to peer.

So, remember you can never lose something that refuses to go away, and be assured that your spirit would never desert you, nor let you wander in the wrong direction or ever go too far astray.

Lake Charles, LA
No different than your lost love ones, your spirit is
never any further than just a thought away.

I believe my being a good dad will not be solely defined or limited to what I was able to do for my family in this lifetime. And though my Dad did so much for all of us, that's not what really stands out.

For I pray that my love ones will remember me much the same as I think of him and recall that just like my Dad, how and why I did what I did to be much more important than all that I somehow managed to do.

San Antonio, TX
By now, you know how I feel about my Dad. I can only pray my
sons will feel even somewhere near the same for me.

One Last Chat

I'm often puzzled as to how my Dad gets me to draw together totally unrelated streams of thought and then somehow compile them all into one. As I sat wondering about this, he reminded **6** me of something else.

Not only did he and I seldom disagree, but thankfully on those rare occasions when we did, we were always able to part with both love and respect still deeply embedded in our hearts.

Years

I know this may sound a bit strange, but oh how I pray he and I could do nothing more than spend a few moments together to simply chat, and yes, even if that meant we'd disagree a time or two.

April 14, 2004
Omaha, NE
For to have but one more face-to-face talk with my Dad, even if ever so brief,
I would do absolutely anything. Did you hear that God ... anything!

I don't know how someone who knowingly does harm to another is unable to see how they're actually harming themselves just as well.

If the truth be told, there are few amongst us who can claim to have lived a life so pure and untainted that they absolutely have never harmed another or just hurt one's feelings, even if it was done with the slightest of intent.

Seattle, WA
We're quick to "do unto others ..." but all too often, and just as sadly,
not always "as we would have them do unto us."

Those whose heart has yet to experience the loss of a love one know not how very hollow, empty, and lonely life can become.

I can't recall a single day to have gone by where something didn't happen to cause me to think of my Dad.

July 4, 2004
Monroe, LA
Celebrating our grandson's very first birthday caused me to wish
his Great Paw-Paw were here to see, hold, and love him.
Happy Birthday, Gabe!

Tears born of pain slowly seep down to settle deep in the bottom of one's heart, leaving unseen paths for all those yet to follow, by keeping them together and from ever getting lost.

September 21, 2004
Council Bluffs, IA
Mom, I'm sorry, but I won't be home for your birthday,
but I'll see you tomorrow. So, have a Happy
Birthday till I get there!

A Gift to Remember

My Mom just gave me the greatest compliment and birthday gift I could ever pray to have received.

She explained that every time she hugs me, it's just like holding on to my Dad; that every time I laugh, she can hear him laughing, and that when I smile, the twinkle she sees in my eyes is the very same as she remembers seeing in his.

September 22, 2004
Just knowing that my Mom thinks of me in these ways has helped to restore
some of the faith I've lost in myself. And although I made it home today
for my birthday, I'm leaving again tomorrow.

Mourning is the one thing that you'll need not set any time aside for, as it'll absolutely and assuredly take all that it needs ... and then a whole lot more.

Denver, CO ~ Airport
Those who are grieving know this to be true, and those who aren't
will one day come to know just how true this is.

Parallel Lives

Recently, while having some medical tests run, I found myself seated in a nuclear medicine waiting room where I knew my Dad had been far too many times. Repeated thoughts of him and what he too was going through filled my worried mind.

Then, a more bothersome series of thoughts began to bombard me: Did he feel as helpless and vulnerable as did I? Did he sit right where I sat, and did he think of me, as I now do of my sons? And were his only concerns for his love ones, not himself, as are mine?

There was a certain tone I detected in my Dad's voice each time I would ask him how was he doing, or if his tests had turned out okay? It wasn't till last night when once again I heard those very same questions, but this time it was my sons asking them of me. Before I could speak, my Dad spoke for me by having me tell them that I was okay and doing just fine; irregardless of what my test results might have shown.

I not only got to hear the one voice I dearly long to hear, but he erased any and all doubt as to my lingering fear. Once again, my Dad taught me what I should have long since learned: that with my sons loving me as much as I do him, there's no longer any reason to ever be concerned.

West Jefferson Hospital

Yep ... He was there!

As a pleasant interruption to an otherwise worrisome day, while I was checking in with the facility's receptionist, she said, "So, you're back?" When I told her I hadn't been there before, she said, "You sure? I'm pretty good with names. I remember the spelling of this one. It's a little different." All I could think to say was "Well, my Dad's been here, but that was years ago." She then said, "Hell, do you know how long I've been here? Could he have come by recently without you knowing it?" I couldn't help but smile and say, "I guess so, with him you just never know!" She then said, "I'm telling you; I remember him!" I then ended a conversation I really didn't want to end with "Yeah ... so do I."

Reality is sometimes enlightening, too often cruel, and as obvious as it is permanent, but the one thing that it's never ... is wrong!

December 25, 2004
Spending Christmas with Mom makes it all that it can possibly be.
Merry Christmas, Dad, with love from the both of us!

He Alone

One's devotion to a higher power is not based simply upon what they publicly profess to so passionately believe. And true faith is not proven by what one claims to have accomplished or even says they're willing to do in the name of the Lord.

For the keeper of the hereafter is both deaf to and unmoved by what one merely proclaims to have said and done; especially when He knows their heart was seldom the driving force behind their words or deeds.

Just as it was always meant to be, we will ultimately be judged upon what He alone knows we truly believe and actually did, as opposed to what we claim to have believed and declare to have done.

January 12, 2005
Omaha, NE
Oddly, this grew from being asked my opinion on the term "devotion."
PS: Happy Birthday, Dad!

Good Conflicts

The difference between disagreeing and rebelling has nothing to do with any opposing opinions or positions. Rather, it has everything to do with the degree of respect we have and show to each other during such occasions.

Though my Dad and I may have disagreed a time or two, the thought of rebelling never entered my mind, and played absolutely no role in any conflicts or even slight differences we ever had.

Being able to look back at such times, knowing we always parted with love in our hearts, allows me to now visit with my Dad free of any conflicting afterthoughts.

Chicago, IL
Which is nice, and something you might want
to remember and strive for.

Had I been with you when you breathed your last breath, I don't believe I could have taken another.

For what reason would I have had?

Too Deep for Me

I've been told that it's possible to scientifically analyze and psychologically scrutinize all that I try to hide deep down within me, even to a finite degree.

However, I challenge you to peer into just one of my tears, and then, please tell me ... what it might be that you think you see in me.

Albuquerque, NM
Then, and only then, will I really care to
hear what you have to say of me.

Words, no matter how well chosen, fail miserably at soothing the pain that **7** lingers on in our heart after losing either a love one or even a very dear and cherished friend.

Since I don't believe that God ever intended for words alone to be **Years** able to express such indescribable sorrow and loneliness, then what makes me think I should even try?

April 14, 2005
Westlawn Cemetery
With this being the 7th year since my Dad's passing, I will no longer
view that number to be the lucky one it's believed to be.

Somewhere Else

Even when you're with love ones, there are times when you're really not with them. You know what I mean; for whatever reasons your mind and your heart are just off somewhere else.

This happens sometimes when I'm playing with my grandkids, for I begin to wonder where someday they might be and just how often will they be thinking of me.

For once my time has passed and they too are off somewhere else, they can rest assured I'll be tagging right along and all they'll need to do is ask me to join in.

Dallas, TX ~ Airport

Not So Sorry

When true remorse drives us to say we're sorry for one's loss, and we truly are, both hearts will be comforted, as they will then share in their mutual pain and despair.

However, there are far too many who offer up hollow condolences knowing them to be insincere, for much like their deceitful words, in their hearts they're not as sorry as they falsely appear.

While at a friend's funeral, I happened to overhear another coworker telling his sons just how very sorry he was for their loss.

It wasn't until this individual walked away that I could see how cold and unaffected he actually was; only then did I realize just how sorry of a person he truly is.

I now see that three types of people attend funerals: those who are there because they truly care, those who feel obligated to be there, and those who wished they could have come up with a good enough reason to give when later asked why they weren't there.

So, which of these are you?

Houston, TX
During this funeral, I'm sorry to say, I had more than one
conversation with more than one supposedly "sorry"
person I thought I knew, but now wish I didn't.

One More Thought

It's only now that I understand why words like "I'm sorry" have evolved to depict so much more than just one singular emotion.

Houston, TX
Okay, now I'm sorry ... so I'll be quiet!

Love can magically change a dark day into one that's bright, simply by taking the lonely chill out of an empty bed on a cold winter's night.

August 3, 2005
Just trying to express one of the many ongoing fears and concerns
I continue to have for my Mom now living without my Dad
PS: Happy Birthday to my love, Pat!

Why is it usually only after it's too late do we regret not having treated the precious time we spend with love ones as the treasured gift and blessing it truly is?

On the one hand, doing so won't cause their eventual departure to be any less for our hearts to bear. Then, on the other, by spending more time together we won't lose what we would have otherwise lost.

Time teaches us that there's a lot more to caring than just simply saying or acting like you do.

September 21, 2005
Though I tried my best, again, I couldn't make it home in time
to be with my Mom on her birthday, so I called her while
I was traveling to wish her a happy one.

Denial

Living in denial is a whole lot easier than dealing with the harsh, uncertainty of the truth, which is why we readily do so, so often.

Only by denying one's passing, a life we silently prayed to be everlasting, do we feel any sense of relief from such sorrow, guilt, and never-ending grief.

Believe me, when you can take no more, you'll eagerly succumb to denial's warm embrace over the cold, stark reality of a love one's mortality, for let there be absolutely no doubt ... that's exactly what I did.

If you stop to think about it, denial is nothing more than an emotional pardon we grant ourselves. We do so to lessen a self-imposed penance that, if we're not careful, will evolve into a lifelong sentence.

Though denial does have its immediate rewards, the personal, ongoing costs are high. The price we pay will continue to rise each day until we're able to set such torment aside, for then and only then will our need to deny finally begin to quietly subside.

Ultimately, denial is our spirit's way of protecting us by secretly allowing our love one's memory to stay fresh and alive. And because it's so deeply embedded in our hearts, true love never parts, with our mutual affection being destined to forever survive.

September 22, 2005
Spent my birthday visiting with my mom and doing
some rebuilding following Hurricane Katrina.

A Common Bond

While going to visit with my Dad, I walked past a child and his mother, who were also visiting with a departed love one. Each had a hand pressed gently upon the headstone while they quietly shed and shared tears that only come with true, heartfelt losses.

My first thought was to quietly bid them a good morning, but I already knew that for the three of us it neither was, nor would it be. So, as my eyes met with the young lady's, I simply nodded my head in regretful response to our mutual, common bond of loss.

As I stood just a few feet from them, I could hear the young mourner mumbling over and over how much he wanted his Daddy to come back, asking why he couldn't, and crying harder and harder with each tear-filled unanswered plea.

I silently asked my Dad to go encourage this young child's father to visit with his son, as we do, and just as often. It was then when I also realized you don't have to be so young to miss and want your Daddy to come back.

Westlawn Cemetery
Grief has no regard for one's age, and cares not
for what our hearts are unable to bear.

It saddens me to see how some hearts hurt so deeply, while at the very same time and faced with the exact same reasons, others are moved so little ... if at all.

It troubles me even more to know that for one to not feel any sense of loss, their hearts had to have lived a life practically void of any love. Sadly, and likely, they failed to develop the desire and ability to feel any sympathy because they too were denied the love that breeds such human emotions. In ways they never let another see, their hearts are being moved; it's just for other reasons.

Then, who am I to try and determine the level of another's pain? For if one chooses to defiantly hide it, while the other openly displays it, are they not then just very different sides of the same coin?

Reno, NV ~ Airport
Long flights make for even longer, often quite diverse conversations
with some revealing and sharing equally deep thoughts.

For Love of Family

What else could there possibly be to look forward to if we didn't have faith that our departed love ones are still watching over and patiently waiting for us? Without that ongoing spiritual reassurance, I fear no day would be any different or more important than another.

If this is as I've said and believe, then why on one day do I write such optimistic, forward-looking things, then by that very evening my words reflect that I truly care not if another tomorrow ever comes? The only thing I can figure is I'm either still in denial, or maybe I'm just more human than I give myself credit for.

The one certainty in my life and the only thing that gets me from one day to another is the love of my family. Their unwavering support, along with the Almighty's forgiving perseverance, is what drives me to do for them what my Dad did and continues to do for me.

So, if I too can inspire my love ones to look forward to not just the rest of today but to all those yet to come, my heart will then be comforted. I pray my words also serve to reassure my Dad just how very much I love, miss, and appreciate him as well.

October 3, 2005
Salt Lake City, UT
Visiting with my oldest son, Craig, on his birthday, and thinking of how empty life would be to not believe this to be true.
Happy Birthday, my son!

The love and respect of family and friends is without question our most valuable of worldly possessions.

Though we know this to be true, these are also the two intangibles of life that we tend to push to their limits and test the most!

November 24, 2005
Today is just another one of those days where nothing felt right, nor did it feel like it was going to get much better. After leaving my Mom's, I sat and sulked, then I remembered my Dad saying, "If there's no really good reason for either doing or not doing something, we clearly have the time to go and do what we should be doing." And with this being Thanksgiving, I knew I needed to go back and simply spend some more time with my Mom ... so, that's just what I did.
Happy Thanksgiving, Dad.

Selfishness

Soon after I lost my Dad, like so many others, I too prayed for God to take me as well. I've since come to realize just how selfish that was of me to be thinking of no one but myself.

Sure, I could easily come up with a whole host of explanations for feeling this way, but none would begin to justify my setting aside the well-being of those who rely upon and love me as I did my Dad.

In my despair, I didn't take the time to think of how I was asking God to impose upon my love ones the very same pain I find myself continually praying to go away.

As is usually the case, my wise and ever-faithful spirit once again intervened. It simply reminded me that if God had intended we live our lives solely for ourselves, He would have never given us any love ones with whom to share it. So, since He did, we must continue to do for others just as others have done for us.

December 25, 2005
Waco, TX
Dad, I can tell how much Corey really misses you, especially during each of the holiday seasons, for when we speak of you the pain I see in his eyes is the same I feel in my heart.

Our Senses

The human weaknesses we must forever contend with beyond the conflicting emotions of love and hate, truth and lies, are our ingrained senses of both guilt and relentless remorse.

Whenever, or if ever, we place too much or not enough emphasis on any of the first four, the last two will assuredly come back to bite and haunt us all the more.

Omaha, NE
The best you can ever hope to do is to briefly try to set guilt and remorse aside until you just learn to live and cope with it.

One's Conscience

Our conscience is quite confounding, for it is as loving as it is devious and ever so conniving. On the one hand, it creates veiled views of reality, obscuring the truth to protect our hearts. Then, on the other, it entices us to conceive hurtful thoughts by imposing painful images where none had existed.

As it silently bores down into the deepest pit of your heart, it slowly drives a rock-hard wedge between you and your soul. And it'll do all this right before lifting your emotions to their highest peak of blinding euphoria.

Your conscience has learned to quietly seduce your spirit into thinking you either did absolutely nothing wrong, or there's nothing else you could have done. And it's quick to do a flip-flop by implanting doubt and uncertainty, causing you to question your every move.

Then, just when you're beginning to feel a slight sense of relief, it'll tease what feelings remain with waves of elation, only to make more room for endless conflicting bouts of regret and grief.

Though our conscience is what often keeps us on the straight and narrow, it'll also head us off in varying directions. Sometimes, while appearing to act in our best interest, it sets us out upon challenging and twisted paths we only later realize and prefer we hadn't traveled.

Fort Worth, TX

My thoughts on the word "conscience."

Maybe it's just me, but I've got a real problem with the way the word "conscience" is pronounced compared to how it's spelled. Really ... look at it.

I will always remember the very first time I ever came across this word. Already knowing how to pronounce the syllable "con" and the word "science," all my third grade mind did was simply merge what I thought I already knew.

Well, you can figure how that went over. Regardless of what I've been taught, I still hesitate each time I read or write this word and would prefer to pronounce it as "con–science," the way I believe it should be.

However, my grammatical conscience has kicked in and although I say and use what's both expected and accepted, it's one of the few words that makes me smile each time I come across it.

So, I guess I better move on to more important things before my literary conscience starts to bother me. Hey, everybody is entitled to their own opinion.

No Longer

Following the passing of a love one, many of the things that you once took for granted will no longer be there to see, feel, or even hear.

Silence will no longer embrace you; instead, it'll haunt and rudely awaken you.

The dark serenity you seek each night will only grow darker and no longer seem to be so quiet and tranquil.

And just a few of your many friends who gave you additional time to emotionally breathe will stop being so sympathetic. At some point, some will feel you should no longer have the need for such a long reprieve.

However, if you'll wait until that somber day when a love one of theirs passes away, you'll quickly see how these naysayers will cease to scorn, for just like you they too will be begging for more time to mourn.

Through our mutual losses everyone will finally come to see and believe the untold value surviving love ones experience when they're allowed to forever grieve.

Atlanta, GA ~ Airport

Ill-Prepared

I now see that not all experiences in life can be taught or explained, as some are but a small part of a very narrow path we must travel solo and learn as we go.

During a conversation with my grandson, as he sat in my lap he asked, "Hey ... Paw-Paw. My Daddy told me that your Daddy passed away. What's passin' away?"

In those next brief but awkward moments, it dawned on me that the **8 Years** answer he sought was a lesson of life I was emotionally ill-prepared to teach him.

I felt that no matter how well and thoughtfully I tried to answer him, this was clearly something he wouldn't comprehend until one day he'd come to learn its true meaning firsthand, and in an equally sad way.

April 14, 2006
Amarillo, TX
Thankfully, he then became distracted and ran off to play.
Happy Birthday to Hunter and Hailee in a few days.

There's a special place for those who stand up for others who can't, and yes, even for those who won't.

With hearing my Dad say this many times, I see how very blessed I am to have two sons that chose to follow the path he clearly laid for them.

Some More Thoughts on Grief

True grief is a life-altering emotion. At some point, with very few exceptions, it will touch every survivor's soul. Though everyone handles grieving differently, I believe it's possible to meaningfully share such deep sorrow only with another whose heart has already suffered that same depth of pain and anguish.

Those who have not yet experienced true grief are, by no fault of their own, ill-prepared to express anything more than thoughtful sympathy for another's loss.

I believe it to be disingenuous for one to feign feeling another's pain if they too have never, ever felt the same.

Just thinking of both my Dad and all the survivors of 09/11.

The only stories I find myself driven to repeat are those littered with treasured, emotional memories my heart longs to share and forever keep.

Oh, what tales I have of my Dad that I can't wait to tell all of his great-grandkids.

I can only pray I don't run out of time before that of words or even my desire to share them.

Westlawn Cemetery
My Dad just assured me that I won't.

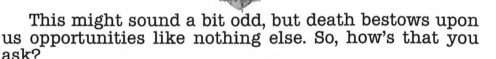

This might sound a bit odd, but death bestows upon us opportunities like nothing else. So, how's that you ask?

Well, tell me, how else will you get to see what Heaven is like and be reunited with your departed love ones? Then, I guess if you're worried about which way you might be going you may very well have reasons to question this.

September 21, 2006
With it being my Mom's birthday, I spent most of the day with her before going to visit my Dad. As another funeral was being conducted, I was reminded of what I've lost, and all that they are yet to face.

One and the Same

Feeling compelled to apologize for possibly having misled you, I began to compose what I felt would be a descriptive distinction between what my Dad inspires me to write and the words I somehow choose to use.

It took me quite a while before I realized that what I was attempting to explain was nothing more than a rewording of what I'd already tried to say. I can't blame my heart for doing what it's compelled to do, which is to echo the many thoughts and feelings my Dad now shares with me?

I gladly accept that there's no difference between what I write and that which he inspires me to feel, or even think, as it's clearly his words alone that I proudly choose to use.

Each time my pen hits the page, I thank God for blessing me twice over. First, He allows my Dad to speak to and through me, and secondly, He then graciously allows me to openly share his words with you combined with that of mine.

September 22, 2006
When I reminded my Mom that it was my 55th birthday she said,
"Damn, I can't believe you're getting that old. Happy Birthday!"
So, to make it an even happier one, I also visited my Dad.

I see where I often use writing as a crutch, for it allows me to briefly rest and lean upon words that my heart can neither muster nor have the courage to speak.

With each word I thank the Almighty for allowing my Dad to help guide me through this never-ending spiritual maze, and for gracing me with such an exceptional family, which also keeps it from being a lonesome one.

Westlawn Cemetery
Knowing what I want to say doesn't
make it any easier to speak it.

Regret is your spirit's way of secretly enticing you to not repeat the same mistakes all over again.

Shreveport, LA
So, I suppose it's best that I start listening more
closely to what it's trying to tell me.

Lose Something?

Whenever we can't find something we tend to think of it as being lost. However, once you've lost a love one you'll thereafter view losing anything and everything so much differently.

If we misplace material things, we simply fail to look in all the right places to find what we seek.

To truly lose something is when there's absolutely no place left to look for what's missing. And no matter how often or hard you might try, you know in your heart before you even start you're not going to find it ... at least not in this lifetime.

St. Louis, MO ~ Airport
The passion in this message is in the meaning it conveys and tends to choke me up
each and every time I read it. But, oddly enough, it came to me while watching
a very young lady frantically looking for her boarding pass. As I've said,
the truth is what it is! I'm happy to have no power or any choice
over when or why my Dad chooses to speak through me.

Silence screams louder than any sound ever made by either man or the angriest of beasts.

December 25, 2006
While spending Christmas with my Mom, at one point she got quiet
and said, "You know, Ferdy really liked to dance to that song."
I was moved to ask her to dance, and in some ways, I'm
sorry I didn't, but I thought it best to let her keep
that memory special of just him and her.

Life must go on following the death of a love one, never to be the same, but the same ... nonetheless.

January 1, 2007
Having these kinds of thoughts on New Year's Day gives
me cause to pause as to what's yet to come!

Please ... Don't

Believe me, I don't mind being told "It'll all work out and things will be okay" by someone who once stood where I now stand, for they paid the price and have already gone where I've yet to go.

However, I'll be damned if I don't simply go ballistic on the next fool that tells me something even close to that who I know, for a fact, has yet to lose a single close love one!

Please don't take me wrong; I'll be more than happy to endlessly rejoice with them over their lack of loss, but they best not even attempt to appease or pacify me with their false, token words of clearly insincere sympathy.

The next person who shamefully pets me like a lost puppy needs to be careful, for they're likely to get bitten!

Sorry ... I was just rubbed the wrong way by the
wrong person at the wrong time.

I almost feel compelled to apologize for somewhat repeating myself. However, because many of my words echo the same feelings so closely, I'm left with but to beg your indulgence. In discussing my dilemma with a friend, he commented that he was pleased to see so many different ways to express such heartfelt emotions.

Please understand that trying to restrain my pen is as futile and pointless as is limiting my heart's need and desire to say certain things only once.

Fort Worth, TX

Taking small, slow steps may be a good way to get you started, but it's likely to only get you where you're headed long after you should have already arrived.

Yet, taking bold, aggressive steps isn't the solution either, for they're likely to cause you to quickly bypass or step over many of the things that make getting where you're heading so very worthwhile.

February 9, 2007
Houston, TX
Dad, if you can, please help make sure I get home
for my 33rd Anniversary this evening.

I pray God never gets as angry with me as I was at Him the day He took my Dad away.

Westlawn Cemetery
I'm sorry, God, but with You having lost a love one, Your son,
You've got to know exactly why I felt the way I did.

Needed

One thing I've come to learn is how reassuring it is to not just know that you're needed but to see, hear, and feel that you are as well. Now, from my own experiences, I see where nothing replaces one-on-one, face-to-face loving hugs and well wishes. Though we often treat them as simple greetings or goodbyes, the more my heart ages the more I see how such exchanges truly mean so much more.

If only I would have realized this while my Dad was still here, I would have shown him everything he ever needed to see, told him all he ever needed to hear, and made sure he felt whatever he needed to feel while he could still realize the true depth of my love for him.

A message to my Dad, while at the same
time a silent one to both my sons.

Mixed Emotions

Recently my Mom gave me an old cassette tape with conversations of my Dad recorded on it. Listening to his voice was just as comforting as it was disturbing.

Comforting, because of all the sounds in this world, this is the one I long most to hear.

Disturbing, because words can't even begin to describe what it's like to sit and listen to the one person I so long to embrace, but sadly no longer can.

9 Years

My faith is continually fed by the belief that come one day, I pray to end up where I'll be able to hear my Dad say, "Unlike before, we can now sit and talk, and talk, and talk ... forevermore."

April 14, 2007
Waco, TX
So, Dad, what do you think about Liana, your second great-grandchild?
Tell me, have you ever seen such joy and pride in Corey's face
as when he literally ran out of the delivery room?
Thanks for being here!

Each time you think fondly of a departed love one you not only resurrect their soul but give their spirit reasons to rejoice.

Are we not truly blessed that our hearts can keep our love ones as close as a mere memory or quiet and loving thought away?

Waco, TX
Memories are permanent links to our love ones that can never be taken away.
I can only pray that come one day, I too stir equally pleasant
memories for all of my love ones as well.

Never ever lose touch
with your spirit.

It'll be there for and
with you when no
one and nothing

else

seems to be near.

It tenderly warms
your aching heart
while gently soothing
soothing your troubled soul.

It'll also answer any
questions you have yet
to ask and guide you
even when you know
not where you might
be wanting to go.

Your spirit is simply God's
loving and enduring way of seeing to it that you're never
truly alone.

Bedford, TX
This evolved following a long conversation with a dear
friend's father-in-law and listening to his deep
spiritual beliefs. Thank you, Larry!

To keep our heart from completely falling apart we shrewdly deceive it with little white lies and fool it into disbelieving what otherwise can't be denied.

April 18, 2007
Amarillo, TX
After celebrating Hunter's and Hailee's birthdays, Pat and I discussed,
yet again, our need to move and get closer to our grandkids.

My Bucket List

Do you too have a wish list of more issues that remain unresolved than those which have been fulfilled? Now I'm not thinking or talking about simple, everyday, mundane matters. What I'm referring to are all those deeply ingrained needs or wants that bother your heart so much that you have trouble finding peace by day or solitude even in the darkest of nights.

One problem that plagues me as much as only one other is having my sons and their families live so far away. To be able to see them more often and play a truly active role in my grandkids' lives stands only second to one other wish on my list of true wants and needs.

If you can recall, from my very first entry, I was not with my Dad when he passed away. My heart tells me that just before he closed his eyes for the last time, he looked around hoping to see me; yet, I wasn't there! So goes and grows my lifelong sense of shame and guilt.

My absence, at that very moment, is what tops my list of regrets, and is something neither my heart nor my guilty conscience will ever let me forget. Such mistakes carry a deep penetrating penalty like no other.

The unrelenting anguish I feel for not being where I should have been has become virtually inescapable. It continues to follow me everywhere, invading my idle thoughts and casting a dark ominous shadow over me on even the brightest of cloudless days.

With all my heart, I pray not to leave this life without seeing my sons' loving eyes gazing back at me. But, if this is too much to ask, when my time has come at last, it'll be no one's fault but my own that I too must pass on while being all alone.

I view our separation from our sons, and their families, as the penance that, regretfully, Pat is also having to pay for my absence at a time when me just being where I should have been was all that was needed.

July 4, 2007
Amarillo, TX
And yes, yet again, while celebrating our grandson Gabe's 4th
birthday the idea of moving closer so we can become a
more integral part of their lives is one item on my
bucket list I pray to one day achieve.

If You Feel Alone

To be alone you really need not be by yourself. In fact, feeling a true sense of loneliness, even when you're in a crowd, is your heart's way of reminding you that there's a lot more to being alone than just simply feeling alone.

Though others may be all around you, you'll know you're truly alone when it's only your voice you can hear, and you alone are the only one that's paying any attention to what you're saying.

September 22, 2007
Corpus Christi, TX
And even though it doesn't sound like it, I'm really having
a happy birthday as I'm spending it with
my first granddaughter!

When I look in another's eyes only to see the same hurt and pain gazing right back at me, our hearts become one, no different than the moon and the stars as they patiently await the setting of each day's sun.

October 3, 2007
Amarillo, TX
After my son Craig's birthday party, I had a long conversation with
his father-in-law, Jessie, who also lost a true love one.

Saving Grace

Within seconds of losing a love one, or even a dear friend, we'll find ourselves aimlessly pacing in the dim shadows of confusion.

It's not until the Almighty knows we're finally ready to once again feel and embrace the sun upon our face will He grant us the ultimate gift of His divine, saving grace.

Spring, TX
Trust and be patient, my friend, for when such a time comes for you,
you too will be ill-prepared, but oh so ready for its arrival.

Death robs us of much more than just our love ones.

Atlanta, GA ~ Airport
My heart hurts whenever I think of my Mom
having to be at home ... all alone.

Here

My Dad is no longer here with me only because of how "here" is so narrowly defined. In spite of that I take great comfort in knowing how he's really here with me, now, in so many more ways than ever before.

November 22, 2007
Spending Thanksgiving with my Mom and, yes, my Dad; sharing
good old tales and stories about happier times gone by.

Time is absolutely the only potion that lessens the pain of absence.

Though I still think of my Dad just as much, if not more, it's only because time has eroded my emotional defences that I'm now able to conceive what I once refused to believe.

The reality of his passing has taught me that the time we spend with love ones only becomes truly important once they and our time together have both expired.

December 25, 2007
Corpus Christi, TX
With that said, this is just one of many holidays I pray to spend with my family
and grandchildren, but oh, how wonderful it would be if my Mom, and
yes ... my Dad could join us during such visits!

Two things I can't control: How much or if others will come to accept and love me, and what memories of me will remain in another's heart.

Two things I must learn to control: What I do that causes others to or not to accept and love me, and what actions I take that will determine just how I'll forever be remembered by both my love ones and friends.

January 4, 2008
Dallas, TX ~ Airport
This arose following my overhearing, albeit only but one side, of
a rather harsh and mean- spirited phone conversation.

Words, once spoken, can never be taken back, for what was said will linger on long after even the quietest of utterances can no longer be heard.

This is why we must think twice before we speak: the first time while a thought is just beginning to brew, and the second right before we actually share whatever words that might come to bear.

Omaha, NE
And so goes much of life itself, for when we speak or act without
first giving it some true thought, we become responsible
for a lot more than just what we said or did.

You may not have a second chance if you waste far too much time having second thoughts.

January 12, 2008
Westlawn Cemetery
Happy Birthday, Dad! It's just me.

A Good Exchange

Some of our most profound, spiritual convictions rest upon the belief that death doesn't close as many doors as it opens.

Although I so want this to be true, until I find out for myself, what am I to do? For my faith to be viewed as true and pure, must I then accept something of which my heart is not yet sure?

And if so, then what of you, for have you never thought to ask such a probing question or two?

Houston, TX ~ Airport
I'm forever moved and surprised by questions that arise in the most
unlikely of places, and how my answers create enduring
expressions on equally questionable faces!

The pain I continue to feel having to go through life without my Dad doesn't so much keep me connected to the past as it often prevents me from looking forward to the future.

San Antonio, TX
Another passing thought complicated by the
simple reality of the truth it reveals.

Empty Arms

I can't stop thinking what it would be like to hug my Dad just once more and if only for but one brief moment.

Then, knowing what it was like to have lost him, respectfully, I don't even think the power of God could cause or force me to ever let him go again!

April 12, 2008
Corpus Christi, TX
Celebrating Liana's 1st birthday and helping my youngest son as he prepares to move yet again, but sadly, even further away!

Rare Souls

How is it that some people never take anything more than merely what's theirs to have? Actually, if the truth were told, they're impulsively driven to give back so much more than they ever hope to receive.

They're quick to defend what's right without question or fear, and seek out only the good in others, even of those who may **10** have sought to do them harm.

Before permitting another to needlessly suffer you'll see these rare and noble souls stepping right up front to make sure that it is they, and they alone, **Years** who might be put in harm's way.

You'll never see them waiting to be waited upon, for they're too busy serving others.

God knew exactly what He was doing each and every time He chose to create such an unusually exceptional soul. When doing so, His purpose is just as clear as it is without hesitation or reservation.

With all the possible words at my disposal, I can think none that will appropriately thank the Almighty for choosing and using my Dad to be but one of His many earthbound envoys.

April 14, 2008
Corpus Christi, TX
Even though it was ten years ago today, the call I received that sad, memorable day has yet to stop ringing in my ears.

There's a Price to Pay

It's only through the compassionate intervention of an all-forgiving God, regardless of what you conceive Him to be, will you ever enjoy any true peace of mind and forever be blessed with the presence of your lost love ones for all eternity.

Then, as we drown in waves of regret over the many misdeeds our soul won't let us forget, we pray for clemency from that same all-loving entity who alone knows of our past wrongdoings.

Admittedly, we've all made innocent errors in judgment; some driven by our emotions, and others simply by the heat of the moment. Yet, nevertheless, we will forever repent over those thoughtless incidents that weren't truly meant, even if they were done purely with what we thought to be the best of intent.

And for those who suffer from the mere frailties of being human, I have neither fear nor concern as their spiritual well-being has long since been earned. Yet, others will forever remain overburdened by the pain of their loss as the agony they feel is deeply entrenched in the dark recesses of their suffering hearts.

Instead, it's those who boldly attest to being totally free of both guilt and regret that rattle my spirit to its core. How can one who knowingly does wrong not be made to dance to the tune of a more demanding song? And should not such offenders have a clear and hefty price to pay for all the agony they've inflicted along their ill-gotten way?

Our faith teaches us of a hellish place the souls of the damned must eventually go; though while they're still of this world we quietly pray they're made to pay a potent penance our pious souls won't come to know.

Then, when all is said and done, and these lost souls can no longer run, that fabled "pound of flesh" may yet get collected, as very well it should. For is it not ingrained in our beliefs that the Almighty will fittingly punish the most egregious violators in the very way we silently prayed He would?

Omaha, NE
Clearly, I'm not having a very good day, knowing I should be with my grandson
celebrating his 5th birthday, but I'm not. Happy Birthday, Gabe!

With every breath, I'm blessed to have yet one more opportunity to spiritually speak and visit with my Dad.

August 3, 2008
And may my words never end until I too arrive at mine!
PS: Happy Birthday to my love, Pat!

I'm Sorry for Your Loss

Each time I hear what's become an almost obligatory comment, "I'm so sorry for your loss," the skeptical side of me stirs. With sadly knowing the pain of loss, I tend to question the sincerity of those who I know are yet to experience such agony.

Case in point: After paying my respects to a dear, departed friend, I approached one of his sons hoping to console him, and offered to help in any way I could. While discussing our mutual losses, another long-time friend came over to express his sympathy, or so I thought.

After a few agonizing minutes, because my friend sounded as cold and insincere as he appeared, the young mourner managed to make a polite excuse and left. With that said, I remained behind so he and I could continue talking. Being an observer to what had just occurred, my bothered and curious mind had to ask, "I'm sorry, but did you also recently lose someone?"

Quite bluntly, and in the same dull, monotone voice I had just witnessed, he unassumingly said, "No, not really; at least not that I know of. Why do you ask?"

At that point, rather than blurt out the harsh admonishment my heart truly wanted to express, I simply replied, "No real reason. I must have just misunderstood you."

It took all I had to keep from saying, "I know you meant well, and I believe you when you say you're sorry, but it must be really difficult to shamelessly share a mournful emotion that neither you nor your heart have yet to experience. It hurts me to say this, but I'm sadder for our friend's son than I am happy for you!" The next few minutes before going our separate ways were quite uncomfortable, to say the least.

(Continued)

So, instead, I opted to make some kind of remark as to him not really knowing how lucky he was, and quietly walked away. But, before I could get out of earshot he sarcastically replied, "So, I guess you think that by my not losing anyone makes me lucky?"

Fortunately, for all concerned, he then turned and walked away before I could gather my thoughts enough to say what my heart was seriously struggling not to bark out at him.

Mothe's Funeral Home

My sincere apologies...

I'm embarrassed for having to admit this, but I owe my dear friend a sincere and truly heartfelt apology for not only having prejudged but totally misjudging his intentions. You can rest assured; when, I see him again, I will tell him so myself.

A few days following my departed friend's services, I was relating the above conversation to another close, mutual friend. It was then when I learned that this ex-coworker had, in fact, neither seen nor spoken to either of his parents since his early teens as he was raised by an aunt and uncle. Though his mom and dad have not yet passed, for all intents and purposes, to him they did long ago.

The more I thought about his hopeless situation, the more I've come to believe that his type of loss is more likely to be much worse, for it's one in which he can't yet mourn and possibly never will.

I suppose losing one's parents to God could be considered a blessing when compared to having literally lost them long before you ever really lose them.

My friend, if you're reading this, I'm sure you'll know it is you to whom I'm referring. Now, more than before, I can't forget that difficult day, and our even more difficult discussion. Please accept my sincerest apology for having both mistakenly and wrongly thought bad of you.

And yes, I'm truly sorry for your premature losses as well.

Just like our fingerprints, no two hearts are exactly the same, further making us unique amongst all others.

Likewise, if either of these two distinctive differences ever ceases to differ us from each other, then, neither will continue to define who we are, once were, or even who we're yet to become.

September 21, 2008
Though I'm leaving in the morning, I managed to stay home long enough to celebrate my Mom's birthday today.
Happy Birthday, Mom ... I love you!

Absolutely, having my love ones unconditionally support me in every possible way is the sustaining force that gets me through yet another trying day.

However, there's a side of me I never let them see that despite all their efforts is what will likely bring about the end of me.

September 22, 2008
Shreveport, LA
Having to be away on yet another birthday,
I threw myself a quiet pity party.

The warm embrace of acceptance tempers and soothes our entire being, much like slipping under an old, worn-out blanket on a very cold, dark, and windy winter's night.

October 2, 2008
Amarillo, TX
So, Dad, what do you think about Craig's new son,
and your latest great-grandson, Jacob?

Try not to focus on the absence of a departed love one's physical presence; rather, take full advantage of every opportunity to joyfully celebrate their ever-present spiritual essence.

October 25, 2008
Lancaster, PA
Well, I guess I need not to tell you, but Corey and Kara
just gave you yet another great-grandson, Logan!

I hope all my prayers somehow manage to help keep my sons from making the same mistakes as did I.

December 25, 2008
Dad, if you would, please visit with Mom as often
as you can, for she misses you so very much.
We both wish you a Merry Christmas!

Though time seems to be ever so slowly soothing the pain of my Dad's absence, I clearly don't have enough time left to where the pain will completely go away.

December 31, 2008
Hey ... Happy New Year, Dad!

Been There ... Done That

If you too ever get to the point where time all but stops, and you become resigned to the fact that each new day is nothing but a prelude to a gloomier tomorrow, I caution you to seek some help.

If your life seems to regress with each new step, and you view the setting of that very day's sun as but another reason to further retreat, I suggest you talk to someone soon.

If your nightly prayers end with a similar plea, one that begs the Almighty to set you free, you might want to seriously pursue some spiritual guidance as well.

Because sad people often make such compelling companions, please don't make the convenient mistake of surrounding yourself with others who are equally depressed and despondent. They will drain you of what little faith and solace you've managed to hold on to, and further burden your already heavy heart.

By now, you've got to know that I support everyone doing all they can to help others get through their despair by bearing some of the load they alone cannot carry. I sincerely hope my words have helped to serve that purpose for you or a love one.

I also pray you come to see, as I am just beginning to, that there's another avenue to follow in how we cope with both life and death. If we treat every breath as a reason to rejoice with our surviving kindred souls, together we can all learn to not fear and to better mourn our own eventual departures as well.

Nothing soothes a hurting heart like the understanding warmth of another's caring embrace. After reading the above entry, the love of my life gave me a hug, and then asked that I seriously try taking some of my own advice.

More Questions

To question one's own faith should not be taken as a sign of having doubt, or even being guilty of disbelieving. Instead, such religious curiosity only serves to show that one's heart, though still vulnerable, is continuing to reach out and grow.

The good Lord openly encourages us to question Him regarding anything of which we're yet uncertain, for He knows His words will quiet our fears while, at the same time, help to lift any heavy or daunting burdens.

It is at conflicting and troubling times when the Almighty intercedes to both provide and reaffirm the answers we so desperately seek.

So, worry not if you find yourself having doubt, or even feeling a bit unsure, for the Lord already knows the true depth of your love and will lovingly accept even those who aren't yet so pious or spiritually pure.

Houston, TX ~ Airport
Once again, I was talking to a curious old soul that's just looking for someone to listen.

I realize I said something close to this before, but these words were spawned by a completely different set of emotional circumstances.

Ultimately, we'll be judged not so much by what we claim to say and do, or by what we led others to believe and wrongly perceive as to the roles we played in this life.

Instead, what we've actually said and done will be reviewed by the only one who knows the absolute truth. As it was meant to be, it is He alone who will decide where for all eternity we will forever reside.

So, some may very well need to take heed, for it will be their true actions that will ultimately rise well above all their false promises, words, and deceitful deeds.

Houston, TX ~ Airport
While waiting on my next flight, this guy next to me was loudly bragging to a rather young lady about all he owned and could do. If he would have given her a brief chance to speak, I think all she would have asked was for him to go sit somewhere else!

No matter how many years a love one has been gone, as each new one comes to pass it feels like an entire lifetime since that of the last.

Please understand, it doesn't get any easier, nor should it.

Tragedy comes quickly, never leaving you as you were, and forever altering all that you pray to one day become. You can never be the same, for you are no longer the same.

The loss of a love one creates high peaks and deep valleys that can neither be cleared nor climbed. Then regret creeps in to drain your heart of any peace of mind that struggles so hard to remain behind.

April 12, 2009

Lancaster, PA

With but a brief smile and tight loving hug from my precious 2-year-old granddaughter,
Liana, she just changed a bad day into the kind I can only pray never ends.
Happy Birthday ... my little bundle of love!

A Matter of Fact

No, Dad, I'm not okay! Sadly, and all too often, life doesn't seem to matter **11** all that much anymore. My fear is if, or when, life begins to once again matter, by then it might just be too late for any of it to really matter anymore.

Years

April 14, 2009

Lancaster, PA

Okay, I'm feeling somewhat down again, but if 11 years hasn't helped
the pain to at least begin to subside ... what the hell will?

I've tried to explain grief in so many ways because it's a word that I find not easy to define. For quite often the very verses I use to depict such sorrow, by their nature, evoke even deeper and more hurtful emotions.

Also, with grief being like so many other similar feelings of loss, I've come to view them like stepping into a room covered in mirrors. For no matter which way I turn or look, all I see is my grieving self, gazing at my confused self, just from a different angle. And no matter how much or hard I stare, I still see nothing more than the same me looking right back at the same old me.

Los Angeles, CA ~ Airport

All I really want to do is simply get home. With as much
as I now travel, simply returning home has
become as joyful as leaving is difficult.

A Life Without Living

When times are good, fantasies of living forever tend to cross everyone's mind. However, the more I ponder over this, the more I've come to see that only a truly heartless person would genuinely desire to live for so very long.

Living forever would provide an unlimited reign of terror for anyone wishing to harm others, yet conversely, for those who do nothing but good, forever won't be enough time to finish or even begin to satisfy all their life's desires.

Knowing the inevitable and unavoidable fate that awaits everyone who ever meant anything to me, I have no desire to forestall my own demise. I simply can't imagine what it would be like to continue on after the passing of all those who made life worth living. This thought alone gives me more than enough reason to both accept and embrace my eventual departure.

I truly don't believe God ever intended for any of us to live beyond our allotted time either without purpose or absent all of our love ones who will have, by then, sadly left us behind.

Dallas, TX ~ Airport
At that point, what would there really be to live for if all
that and those we cherished are no longer there?

Time has shown me that there's an indescribable difference between never did, never would, and doing all the things you never should.

Houston, TX ~ Airport
Since there are no more flights out tonight, I'm stuck here until
tomorrow, but I'll make it home for my Mom's birthday.

Listening

It's taken me this long to finally understand the true despair and disappointment I both felt and saw in my Dad's eyes when I failed to listen to all he was trying to tell me.

It's not that my sons don't listen to me; it's just that they don't seem to listen any better than I did.

September 21, 2009
New Orleans, LA ~ Airport
Still scrambling to get home for my Mom's birthday.
So, don't get started without me! And yes,
I leave again tomorrow on mine.

A true loss will sober you like nothing else.

For the reality of having a love one taken away will serve as a continual, menacing hangover to which there is no miracle elixir or next-day, morning-after cure.

September 22, 2009

Ontario, CA ~ Airport

Well, last year the same thing occurred; I made it home for my Mom's birthday but left the next day on mine. And yes, I knew this would happen before planning this trip!

No matter how closely you listen, you'll never hear the song being played by another's heartstrings.

Yet, if you look close enough you'll get to see the melody that's reflecting in their eyes.

October 2, 2009

Amarillo, TX

This thought arose while talking with my son Craig's father-in-law, Jessie, about our mutual losses. Now, back to why we came here; Happy Birthday to Jacob today and Craig tomorrow!

In watching how others cope with the loss of their love ones, I'm often amazed at just how much one's heart can endure and absorb when under such duress.

Although we deal with our losses in many different ways, there are common threads that seem to be interwoven throughout these emotional forfeitures: We all tend to regret what our hearts are unable to forget. We all want to believe that our lost love ones will be waiting for our souls to come through. And looming well above all else, few of us have any doubt that when we get back together with our love ones, it'll be even more wonderful than we could have ever prayed for.

Shreveport, LA

Being on the road yet again, I really didn't see my day getting much better than how it began. However, after speaking with Pat and my two sons the dim light at the end of my tunnel began to glow much brighter.

Nobody should be denied the chance to tell someone they love goodbye, when other than "I love you ... goodbye" is all that's left to be said.

November 26, 2009

Absolutely nothing causes memories of lost love ones to resurface more than holidays.

Happy Thanksgiving, Dad.

There are so many times I pray that my Dad is watching and listening to me, but then there are so many other times when I'd truly be ashamed if he were.

December 22, 2009
Lancaster, PA
So, Dad … what do you think of your latest
great-granddaughter, Lyssa?

Do It

When you try to do something that you really don't believe you can, it's likely to remain undone until you either gain the knowledge and confidence you need to do it, or you humbly accept the fact that you were right before you tried … you just simply can't do it!

December 25, 2009
Lancaster, PA
A rather humorous message from my Dad, who was watching
me fail at doing something I had no business attempting.
Merry Christmas, Dad.

Before you ask questions that challenge another's grieving soul, be careful the answers you seek don't reveal wounds best left concealed or reopen old ones that have not yet healed.

So, instead, pursue only well-thought-out inquiries that gently nudge another's heart. For only through sympathy and understanding will your curiosity quietly go undetected if compassionate answers are all that's being sought.

Then, ask such if you dare, but be cautiously aware that your questions are for no other reason than to show another just how much you sincerely care.

Biloxi, MS
Sitting with some good friends and talking
about all of our mutual losses.

The Flip Side

By now, I'm all but certain that I've clearly conveyed my deep love and respect for my Dad. Though I've told you quite a lot, there's so much more that's still quietly sleeping deep down in the well of my pen.

With that said, I'm not so naïve to think or believe that he's one of those ultra-rare souls who lived a purely virtuous life, one so chaste and unblemished as to not ever be questioned, but who amongst us really have?

Instead of simply denying or even overlooking his weaknesses and vulnerabilities, I accepted them and rejoiced in having learned from how he dealt with his failings. In the long run, he and I fared better due to his genuinely open, earnest, and honest efforts.

January 12, 2010
Houston, TX ~ Airport
This was inspired by a really long conversation I had yesterday with my Mom.
She shared a lot, but the one thing that came through more than anything
else was her continuing love and devotion for my Dad!

The most bothersome questions of the heart often need not be asked; in fact, sometimes it's best they remain kept to one's self. Though doing this may leave you with some doubt, that's a much better alternative than giving another's agonizing soul further reasons to hurt even more.

From what I've personally faced, most questions of me that stirred my emotions were comprise of the very words that form my answers. With that in mind, at such particularly emotional times, I wish others would rethink what they're about to ask, for quite often they'd find themselves quietly answering themselves and not having added to another's already mounting pain.

San Antonio, TX
And remember, not every question asked has to have,
nor will it have, the answer you seek.

My Dad guides not only my heart, soul, and spirit, but obviously every stroke of my pen as well.

Houston, TX ~ Airport
I know I've expressed this somewhat before, but when so moved,
I will do it again, and most probably ... yet again.

To Dad

Well, it's hard to believe that it's been twelve long years since God chose **12** to relieve you of your earthbound pain and problems you faced in those last few years, I find myself unsure whether I should be angry or somehow **Years** strangely thankful for Him having taken you.

I see your passing as an anniversary that we can only truly celebrated with an overdue embrace when the Almighty brings us back together through my demise.

April 14, 2010
Council Bluffs, IA
*My only consolation comes in knowing that though I must wait
patiently for that blessed day, it will come ... or so I pray.*

As it is often with life itself, time also becomes ever so much crueler the slower it passes.

April 14, 2010
Omaha, NE ~ Airport
Just rethinking over a lot of what I've thus far written.

Don't Let It Happen

Seldom do we ever truly appreciate our love ones and friends until we're threatened with the real possibility of either losing them or that of our own passing. Too often we only come to sincerely value those closest to us when such unthinkable tragedies appear upon our horizon.

With that in mind, I suggest you cherish dearly all that you do have while you're still able to share the simple pleasures of life, especially with those who truly give it meaning.

If you feel you should be doing more for a special love one, or an old friend, then I suggest you do so before no more can be done either by you or for them.

Please believe when I say that it'll take but a single regret to cloud a thousand happy memories.

April 18, 2010
Amarillo, TX
*We're creating good memories with two of our grandkids.
Happy Birthday to both Hunter and Hailee!*

The learning process for grieving is much the same as a young bird's first attempt at flying, for they are both compelling challenges that can't be ignored.

Yet, not until both step off into the unknown will they find out if what they've done turns out to be right or wrong.

April 23, 2010
Venice, Italy
Yes, Dad, this place is so very beautiful.

Other than to appease one's own conscience, it's pointless to try and pay respect to a departed love one had you not done so long before a cold and heartless, engraved stone separates the two of you.

April 23, 2010
Florence, Italy
Though I somewhat expressed this feeling before, it resurfaced again as I walked by the many tombs deep down in the Catacombs.

More Thoughts on Tears

Because tears born of joy get happily swiped away, I'll bet that no matter how hard one tries they can't recall what happy tears taste like.

However, tears born of pain go virtually unnoticed. For, regardless of how many we eventually shed, there'll never be nearly enough to douse the flames quietly smoldering in a heart that's still aching and mourning.

On the other hand, tears born of regret have a hollow taste like nothing else, one you'll not soon forget. Then, might I ask ... how does one even begin to describe the taste of empty?

April 23, 2010
Florence, Italy
Tears are God's way of helping you to cleanse your soul.

Until my death reunites me and my Dad, I view each day as but the price I must pay for not appreciating all that I once had.

April 23, 2010
Positano, Italy
This is to let my sons know I will be there for them as well.

Time

There will come a time when time is the one thing we'll no longer have. Material possessions will have lost their value once there's no more time to enjoy them.

Things our hearts were once driven to gather will thereafter cease to matter. And all those overlooked intangibles we never took the time to fully appreciate will slowly become nothing but vague memories and elusive recollections of lost opportunities and occasions.

That's until the day when God sweeps a love one away, for then and ever more will we sadly reminisce over all the good times we missed and unfortunately failed to celebrate before.

Then, at an unknown place and time we'll find ourselves in the ultimate judgment line, and it's there where we'll be reunited to live as one, sitting together and joyfully greeting the rise of each new morning's sun.

April 24, 2010
Amalfi Coast, Italy
If, in my afterlife, I can travel to anywhere I wish, I'll be coming back here.

I see where my words, even if only written to express a fleeting thought, unintentionally revealed something my heart may have actually wanted to keep concealed.

So, now, I find myself having to contend with all those conflicting emotions I tried to keep buried deeply within.

And although there's so many more words still eluding my tear-filled pen, I guess they'll just have to remain, at least for now, both unspoken and unwritten.

April 25, 2010
Amalfi Coast, Italy
I just witnessed what sounded like a good old Italian ass-chewin'. The young girl
taking the brunt of her mother's fury is what prompted me to ponder
the impact of words, even those we may not understand.

Quietly listening intently and sincerely are two of the greatest gifts we can ever give to another, especially during times when they are filled with mournful despair.

April 27, 2010
Isle of Capri, Italy
Sitting on the patio of Andrea's villa looking out at the Mediterranean Sea.
To my dear friend ... we truly can't thank you enough!

Another Time

For those times when you're visiting a resting love one with your head bowed, hands clasped, and you find yourself unable to speak, take solace and comfort in your mutual silence.

And be patient, my friend, for never will you more deeply feel your shared thoughts and words, especially since what's being said need not be heard.

Clearly, both hearts rejoice in spending such quiet times together, knowing the day will come when you'll be reunited, but this time, thankfully … it'll be forever.

April 29, 2010
Isle of Capri, Italy
I love watching my Dad guide my pen as he lays such words onto the page.

Failure to act upon the advice and counsel of your spirit will cause you to endure a lifetime of anguish and agony, while forever chasing after an eternity of regret.

April 30, 2010
Rome, Italy
This one's deeper than the waters we just crossed.

Those who knew my Dad remember him to have been a true artist in every sense of the word. His God-given talents and knowledge of all forms of art gave him a deep appreciation for the gifts of others, especially that of the old masters. For him, their collective works are not likely to ever be duplicated. By this I truly don't wish to disparage the abilities exhibited by many of today's artists, but my Dad views the bar to have been set so exceedingly high that another coming even close to equalling what they accomplished will be a rare feat; albeit ever-pleasingly possible.

So, here I stand amongst the works of these very same ancient masters, wishing my Dad were here to enjoy and share in all that I'm seeing, sensing, and experiencing. Then, it dawned on me: he is here … for he's seeing it through my eyes, just as I'm now viewing it through his.

May 2, 2010
The Vatican ~ Rome, Italy
Clearly, our aching and inseparable hearts have been equally moved and stirred.
It pleases me beyond words to share this unique experience with my Dad.

I find myself in total awe of all the beauty man can create when guided by the hand of God.

May 5, 2010
The Vatican ~ Rome, Italy
Sadly, we're heading home later today.☹

If you ever catch yourself wishing I were still there, or begin to worry that I may no longer be around when you need me, fear not, for I'm always a lot closer than you might think.

In fact, the next time you feel like you've bumped into something with nothing there to bump into, simply say excuse me and go on about your business. Though I didn't mean to ... it was just me getting in your way.

San Antonio, TX
Thanks, Dad, I needed that! I too wish to leave
the same message and legacy for my sons.

If you ever hold your heart, soul, or spirit back for fear of making mistakes, just think how much of life will pass right by you.

September 21, 2010
This came to me while celebrating my Mom's birthday and discussing
some of the things she now wishes she and my Dad had done
while they were still young enough to have done so.

For

The good Lord sees to it that a love one's absence is made a lot less painful by their spiritual presence; for then, no matter where we roam, our conjoined hearts will never really be alone.

It's so comforting that with every beat I'm reunited with my Dad; for I know it's only because of a loving God that reassuring times like this will forever be had.

And because of all this I no longer view Heaven to be so far away as to keep us apart, for anytime I wish to be with my Dad, I need only place my hand over my heart.

September 22, 2010
Sharing what's left of my 59th birthday with my Dad,
and believe it or not, this time I'm home!

Each time memories of my Dad arise, it's much like finding an old, dusty box of misplaced pictures in the attic. I get to both rejoice in its contents and relive so many good times all over again.

I've come to see where my heart is the attic of my soul.

It's yet another of life's cruel realizations that once a love one has passed, we lose not just them but the opportunity to say the many things we failed to say before and will thereafter regret our silence forevermore.

I pray I never run out of ways to say both
I'm sorry and I love you!

It's not until one's spirit experiences the slightest glimpse from the "other side" will they begin to understand just how loud and quiet, full and empty; the very same room can be.

October 4, 2010
Reno, NV ~ Renown Hospital
Being struck down with multiple blood clots in both lungs, my Dad had to have
intervened, as I was told no less than twice, I should have died!

On the morning that I was released, one of my nurses made a remark, "You've either lived a good life or you've got someone watching over you." Before I could respond, she said, "Yeah ... you got that right!"

Since I hadn't said anything, and to my regret didn't hear anything, the only thing she could have possibly heard was the utterings of my Dad. Left with only to imagine what he intended for her alone to hear, I just smiled in agreement and thanked her for both helping me to recover and thoughtful words.

October 7, 2010
Reno, NV – Renown Hospital
Being told I was released sounded good, but not nearly as satisfying as having
my nurse unwittingly let me know my Dad was right there with me.

Both loving and hurting hearts have a language all their own that no one else need hear or understand.

When you're feeling down, go do something good for someone. It'll not only make the both of you feel better, it'll consume some precious time you might otherwise spend feeling sorry for yourself.

Something my Dad said to me on one of his darkest days.

I Feel for Her

While heading home on this Christmas Eve, I was seated next to a rather young lady who appeared to be quite bothered and unsettled. Soon after taking off, she asked me where was I going? As I began to explain that I was heading home, she abruptly interrupted me by saying "So am I." Then, as quickly as she spoke up, her demeanor changed back to that same seemingly sad and deeply troubled person I first saw.

I said nothing more so she could gather her thoughts and calm down a bit. Later, when she looked up at me, I simply smiled and said, "I don't know what you might be facing, but if it helps, know that you're not alone." She paused a second or two and asked, "How would you know? How do you stop from feeling so alone when, for the first time in your life, you are?" I then told her, "If it's a loss you're facing, I've long since been there. At some point you'll come to see that you aren't alone, and even more importantly, you never will be. In time they'll come through to you. Please trust me when is say this."

She then laid her head back and without looking at me softly mumbled, "Apparently, you already know something I don't," to which I said, "Yes, sadly I do. And though it'll take time, please know that one day you too will come to feel, hear, and even accept all that I now do. That's when it'll be your turn to pass this on to another."

December 24, 2010
Airborne and heading home
Tonight, I'll say a quiet prayer for my in-flight friend,
and ask my Dad to seek out whomever she lost.

Sympathy is the one thing you can neither fully nor honestly express without first having personally and sincerely received it from another.

December 25, 2010
Spending Christmas with Mom, and yep ... my Dad as well!

Just like my Dad, I too take great comfort in doing whatever it might be my sons may ask or need of me.

January 8, 2011
Lancaster, PA
After helping one of my sons today, I now know how my Dad
felt when he would help me. Happy Birthday, Corey!

Losing Love Ones

When you lose a true love one you'll quickly offer to trade your soul, and much more, for their return. In a heartbeat, you'll swap places with them, and there's absolutely nothing you wouldn't give to simply spend yet one more single, solitary moment in their embrace.

And no matter what others may say or try to do to comfort you, your pain will remain, all the same.

Even for those who continually show true concern and compassion for their love ones, by no means will their departures be any easier. However, doing so will leave behind a lot less to both mourn and regret.

January 12, 2011
Westlawn Cemetery
Yet another quite and insightful thought
from my Dad, and on his birthday.

For those to whom my messages have thus far neither meaning nor value, I'm tempted to ask that you read no further.

On the other hand, if my words have failed to inspire you to think more of others than of yourself, or of love ones in a more caring and thoughtful way, maybe it is I who should just stop writing.

Denver, CO ~ Airport
I'll bet this is one you never expected!

Losing Others

If the truth be told, no one considers each and every relative to be a true love one. And then, with not all genuine love ones being a relative, our hearts must learn to somehow compassionately discern which is which.

For those who are in doubt as to the true depth of their feelings for another, sadly, it's likely to take their passing before we actually feel the full impact of their influence and presence in our lives via their absence.

So, whether one is a relative, friend, or even a foe, our hearts drive us to mourn the passing of more than only those we know. And though we grieve the loss of friends, some more than others, how can we not grieve the loss of any soul who's touched ours, even if ever so briefly? Then, of those who remain, I'm left to wonder if they will feel the same whenever it becomes our time to go?

Please believe me, unless you begin to treat the precious time you can spend with friends and love ones as being the irreplaceable moments they are, once they're all gone the only ones you'll be left with are all the others you may not wish to embrace.

Tyler, TX
Decisions, decisions ... decisions!

Every year, I dread **13** the coming of yesterday simply because it's the day before today, and by now, we all know what day that is.

Though others can **Years** mourn with you, they can't mourn for you. I've come to see where there are as many ways to mourn ... as there are reasons.

April 14, 2011
Westlawn Cemetery
Not all anniversaries were meant to be celebrated in this lifetime.

Depending upon how wisely we play the hand we've been dealt, our passing will be either forever mourned or eternally forlorn.

Salt Lake City, UT
Life everlasting is the one gamble where everything depends upon so much more than just the turn of the last card.

No Do-Overs

You have no idea how much I wish the following weren't true, but I'm ashamed to say ... it is.

As I previously and poorly tried to explain, because I worked really long hours mostly out of my home office, I sometimes viewed untimely calls and visits by my Dad as being just that. I really tried to not let it show, but I was clearly no better at hiding my impatience back then than are my sons at letting theirs slip through now.

With that said, and my ignorant insensitivity boldly underscored, it goes without saying that there are no words to explain how I would now welcome and treasure each and every such visit or call. They were unparalleled and missed moments in time that no amount of praying can undo or redo. The key words here are "they were," for I can no more go back in time than I can possibly begin to apologize to an engraved wall of stone.

My Dad's absence has unmistakably shown me that there is absolutely no price I wouldn't pay to have him now repeatedly call me in the middle of my busiest day. And if he could stop by to visit, just one more time, my most frequent prayer would then be satisfied.

To look him in the eye and describe how truly sorry I am would lift a menacing veil of shame from my aging, guilt-riddled mind. My only comfort in all of this is knowing that he hears me now, and my sons, upon reading this will learn from my most egregious mistakes.

September 22, 2011
Biloxi, MS
On another note, though it may not sound like it, today is a good day.
I am truly blessed to be spending my 60th birthday with
the love of my life, four of my dearest friends,
and I'm happy to say ... my Dad as well!

Death is a demanding, brutal, and hard taskmaster, for it stands stern over a very special class of students whose attendance is required ... even if only but once.

It's different than any other lesson we'll ever receive, for it's absolutely the only course where no one is even given a chance to fail, neither literally nor figuratively, as everyone who attends is guaranteed to pass.

Pun fully intended!

What I Needed to Hear

My Dad just reassured me by quietly whispering, "In listening to your thoughts and prayers, please know that you need not ever ask or even pray for me to be with or near you ... for just as I am now, I will always be."

Amarillo, TX
October 2, 2011
As will I for my sons, grandkids, and eventually that of theirs.
Happy Birthday to Jacob today and Craig tomorrow!

Don't Bother

It serves no purpose to visit a departed love one if you failed to spend some quality time with them while you still had that blessed chance.

If you find yourself standing before their final place of rest with no true sense of sorrow, I suggest you simply bid them a very respectful goodbye and not return until your heart compels you to do so.

For silence to speak, it must have a clear message that both loving hearts can hear. If you're moved to visit with a resting love one, just remember, it's only the one who's now reclining that has a reason to be so quiet.

November 24, 2011
At Westlawn Cemetery with Mom
Happy Thanksgiving, Dad.

She's lost more than she knows...

With it being Thanksgiving, I took Mom to the cemetery to visit with Dad. While there, I witnessed a young lady standing at the foot of what had to be a love one's gravesite. Clearly, being heartbroken to the point of tears, her anguish was just as real as is the depth of her loss.

To this very day, seeing and feeling another's heart sensing such pain tugs fiercely at mine as well, for all too often, I too arrive and leave here feeling much the same and equally distraught.

However, what hurt as much as seeing her in such pain was how her partner was so visibly unmoved and unaffected by her level of grief-stricken torment. He obviously couldn't wait for her to stop crying simply so they could leave.

I can only pray that her tears kept her from seeing what I did. I also hope she soon comes to realize that he can't truly love her, for to love another you must also hurt along with them, for which he's clearly feels neither.

Anyway ... once again, Happy Thanksgiving, Dad, from the both of us!

Sometimes, it may very well take us going beyond where we personally feel comfortable if we are to truly help others find the lasting relief and consolation they so desperately seek.

To faithfully serve as our brother's keeper we need not only be their daily defender, but more importantly, the emotional custodian of their heart as well.

Christmas Eve

Well, Daddy, with today being Christmas Eve, between your urging and my knowing I needed to, I gladly stayed to share it with Mom. We decided Pat would spend Christmas with Corey and the grandkids, while I remained here. Seeing the kiddos as seldom as I do, I'd be lying if I didn't admit to a part of me wanting to go as well, for I miss being with them much the same as no longer being with you.

As you could see, Mom and I really enjoyed reminiscing and reliving many of the times gone by, for those were the good old days. Christmas was always the one holiday when our entire extended family got together, which I now see was what helped keep us together. However, with my family being separated by both time and distance, not having them close truly bothers me. Though they tell me they love me each time we part, there's something about looking at their smiling faces while they're saying it.

With many of the happier moments we recalled being so memorable, we were often brought to tears, and I could feel you laughing and crying right along with us. Though Mom was telling the stories, in my heart, I knew it was you I was listening to and your words I heard her speaking.

I remember thinking that I didn't want the night to end, but it dawned on me that for me to go home, I would have to leave not only Mom, but you as well. Then, as always, you slipped in and told me what I needed to hear. You let me know you'd be right there with her, and the two of you could then spend some quiet time together. So, with that, a short time later, I reluctantly left.

As it turned out, my staying home with Mom and having you there made this a very, very special Christmas for all three of us.

December 24, 2011
May you have a very Merry Christmas! My next two entries will show any
disbelievers the real reason why you had me stay home with Mom.

Christmas Day

Though many days with my Mom, of late, have been trying and worrisome, today was like few others and I pray not to be a sign of things to come. Though this is yet another Christmas to be remembered, it's not for any reasons I would prefer.

It was a very long day and at times quite difficult. More than enough was going on to where I would have normally been inspired to capture some semblance of what occurred, but I just didn't ... I couldn't. My Mom's condition and state of mind had me way too distracted and concerned to consciously think of much else.

Even with long periods where all I did was sit and watch her sleep, it wasn't until long after being home I realized that I hadn't kept any purposeful notes or even scribbled down brief descriptive feelings of some of today's more memorable moments.

Yet, I knew if I allowed myself some quiet and undistracted time I could recreate much of what went on today. In fact, I did just that, but by the time I got around to doing so, I too was in no state of mind to do justice to either my Mom's situation or the totality of today's events.

I feel I must apologize for not being able to share even a portion of what all went on today, but with it and tonight being so unsettling, I had to allow myself some quiet time for both my heart and my mind to somewhat unwind.

Yet, tomorrow, once I've gotten some rest and I'm able to better gather my thoughts and emotions, I'll try to compose something that begins to reflect a day that I now see needs to be remembered. It's not that I'm at a loss for words, but for the first time in quite a long time, I just feel really lost.

So, please bear with me until at least tomorrow, but for now ... I bid you and my Mom a goodnight.

December 25, 2011
Just trying to get through a day that although it's
ending, it still feels like it had just begun.

Follow-Up to Christmas Day

Well, here I am, but it's the day after Christmas, and I must thank my Dad for getting me out of bed so early yesterday, Christmas morning. At first, I thought I'd just lie back, relax, and think about how good Christmas Eve had turned out. Instead, I felt a disturbing urge to get up, the cause for which I would later learn.

Since I had already prepared a few of Mom's favorite Christmas dishes, thankfully, there wasn't much left for me to do. I must say, the entire time I was getting things together, I could feel my Dad pressing me to stop and go straight to Mom's. So, I quickly finished, packed up what I was doing, and swiftly headed over there. The whole time while driving my level of concern grew. To reassure myself, I thought back to how much we had laughed the night before, and that she seemed to be feeling fine when I tucked her into bed. Now, in hindsight, a sense of guilt plagues me for not staying.

His reasons for getting me there so quickly were as obvious as they were necessary. She was very pale and extremely weak. When I told her she needed to go to the hospital, she refused until I convinced her that it was Dad who wanted her to go. She then said she wasn't going unless he was coming along, to which I told her he was and she responded, "Oh well ... that's good."

Being in the emergency room for the entire day and most of the evening, many more tests were run than answers given. Once we were finally released and managed to make it back home, I warmed us both some dinner. With not eating all day, she ate really well and actually seemed to enjoy it. Soon after, she let me know she was tired and wanted to go to bed. So, only after I made sure she was comfortable and everything was just the way she likes it, I tucked her in for the night.

Obviously, this time I stayed, checking on her throughout the night. Although I heard her tossing and turning a time or two, she seemed to have slept pretty well; I know a lot better than I did.

Lately, she's been asking for my Dad a lot, but this morning her tone was different. "Where's Daddy? Is he still here?" "Yeah, Mom, he's right here." After hearing that, her tone returned to normal, and she said, "Oh, that's good. I'm glad!" As I walked away, I quietly mumbled, "Yes, Mom, that is good, and believe me, I'm glad too. When you're happy ... I'm happy!" To that she smiled and drifted back off to sleep.

December 26, 2011

I've been taught that everything is just part of a greater plan, but if that's so,
I'm really struggling to figure out the meaning behind all of this.

The depth of love and loss for a departed love one is reflected by the scars their absence forever embeds upon our hearts.

Hug 'Em Again

In thinking back to Christmas Day, while in the emergency room with my Mom, I met up with an old friend. After I introduced them and explained why we were there, he told us of a really bad auto accident his younger sister was just in. To be honest, all of this talking served as a good diversion for my Mom. Not only did she listen intently, but she actually became engaged in the conversation and even made some really caring and insightful comments.

It wasn't but a short while later when a heart-wrenching cry came from the trauma room entrance area where a frantic young lady had just emerged. When her eyes met up with my friend's, she headed in his direction. As soon as he saw what I saw, though he looked my way, he wasn't really looking at me, but more like through me. He sighed deeply and nervously shook his head as he embraced her. I couldn't make out what she said, but I didn't need to; her message was as clear as the pain engulfing her face and the tears streaming from her eyes.

Then, when an elderly lady came out to join them, I moved my Mom so they could sit together and comfort one another. Before doing so, I expressed my deep heartfelt sympathy and offered to help in any way I could.

My friend shook my hand, hugged, and thanked me, but as our eyes met, this time I saw something quite different. I could see right through the façade he was trying so hard to portray. I know he was being strong for the sake of his family, but I also knew that this would only last until he could finally be alone with nothing more than his thoughts and cherished memories of his sister.

(Continued)

During all of this, what struck me was how his initial reaction so closely mimicked mine when I first learned of my Dad's passing. Much like myself, he stayed stoic and neither broke down nor shed a visible tear, at least not right then and there. It was just as if I were staring into an obscured mirror and listening to an old script being read from my past.

Though I gave my friend some space, I stayed close by. I simply had to, for I remembered how I felt when I got that same message, and how I wished I had someone with whom to talk. I wanted him to know I was there for him if he needed me.

Yes, his relatives were there, but clearly, none were ready or able to speak without breaking down. So, I simply let him say whatever he felt needed to be said, and listened intently with a supportive ear, as he repeatedly tried to come to grips with the reality of his loss.

As my friend spoke about his sister, I learned that the first young lady was her daughter. Hearing that, I better understood what I detected in her voice just moments earlier. As she tried to convey the loss of her mom, I heard something no one else would have. The sheer pain and trepidation embedded in her voice sounded exactly the same as what I heard coming from Pat when she tried to tell me of my Dad's passing. Not only was this young soul dealing with her own pain and loss, she had to remain strong enough to deliver a message she was clearly ill-prepared to carry.

So, if you're ever around when a friend or love one is in a similar situation, simply listen until they can speak no more. Hug them tightly to let them know you're there if they need you, and then, hug 'em again, but this time don't let go until you feel them … letting go of you first.

January 12, 2012
I hope my friend gets to read this, and if he does, I would ask him to let his
young niece know just how sorry I am for her loss as well.
Also … Happy Birthday, Dad!

It seems that regret is yet another side effect of grief, but time and despair have taught me that all too often it's actually the other way around.

Westlawn Cemetery
Just as opposites attract, I've learned that
upsetting emotions often detract.

Attempting to live a life absent a dear love one is like trying to tell the time with a watch that has only one hand. Though they both may have served their given purposes, neither can now do as they once did so simply and reliably.

Sadly, only but one of the two can ever be mended, for the other's time has eternally ended. Yet, if in our hearts we cherish them just as much as we always did, they will remain all the same, with one giving us half of the right time twice a day and the other faithfully remaining close by our side in every other possible way.

Westlawn Cemetery
Our time together will only truly and forever become
intertwined once I lose what's left of mine.

Traveling gives one time to think, and deep thought provides us with so many reasons to further understand and appreciate all that we had as well as respectfully mourn all that we've lost.

Houston, TX ~ Airport
As you've seen, I travel an awful lot. Though I often regret doing so, there
are times when I welcome the birth of such emotionally provoking
thoughts as this one, in such totally insensitive surroundings.

Dad, you know Mom is becoming more and more absent-minded lately. She's also claiming to see things, friends, and people in the middle of the night, so much so that I'm becoming truly concerned for her.

And yes, she tells me, over and over again, of speaking with you and clearly remembering you visiting with her, night after night. Hell, if I can hear you, and we speak continually through your excerpts to me, then why should I not believe that she also sees and talks with you? However, I must admit, to hear that you're actually spending time with her … now that makes me jealous! ☺

Seriously, why don't you just get Mom to call me the next time you're there; this way all three of us can visit at the same time.

Westlawn Cemetery
Sometimes, I just need to give myself a really good
reason to laugh simply to keep from crying.

Lingering Hopes

Well, it appears Mom is suffering with the onset of dementia. She doesn't remember that you, her husband of fifty-plus years, her sister, parents, and almost every family member of her age have passed away. I guess, in an odd sort of way, that shields her from the sad truth of it all.

It truly doesn't get any easier each time she complains about not having seen them lately and asks if I think they might be coming by. Every time the door opens, she immediately glances over, truly expecting one of them to be walking in. I can't explain how much it hurts to watch her stare so intently, only to look away disappointed. However, through all of this she still remains hopeful, as she often cheerfully remarks, "Well, they're probably on their way and ought'a **14** be gettin' pretty close by now... don't ya' think?"

Please tell me, what **14** should I do when she asks me these things, or even if her mom could stop by to take her back **Years** home? Believe me, just telling her that they'll be here shortly doesn't work, for misdirecting her only delays later constant and repeated questioning of the same. So, I find myself at a loss to explain what it's like to sit and watch her lingering hopes slowly and sadly dissolve. At times I can tell she's still aware enough to have figured out that I'm not telling her the truth, or all she would like to know.

Recently, Mom called me late one night to ask, "Do you think you could come bring me home? I would call Gary, but he never comes by anymore. He doesn't really visit me all that much. It's almost like he's becoming a stranger."

Though I'm aware she doesn't know or mean what she's saying, it still hurts deeply to hear her utter such words. Even the possibility that she might be thinking or feeling this of me cuts deeply into what little remains of my forever faithful, yet worried and now wounded, heart.

Please tell me, how do I compassionately convey to Mom what she can no longer grasp, and in her heart truly doesn't even want to believe? I've learned that by doing what I thought to be right, just how very wrong I can sometimes be.

So, Dad, please tell me, is what I'm doing right for Mom's sake? And, if you would, let her know that in spite of what she sometimes thinks of me how much I do truly love her.

(Continued)

It was fourteen years ago today and Mom was still faithfully taking care of you right up until the very end. Although I know you're doing everything you can to help and comfort her, my primary and chief concern is ... am I?

April 14, 2012
Every time I look at my sons I pray they don't
someday face this same situation with me.

Because I didn't say I love you as much as I could or should have, I now find myself quietly uttering these words each time I visit with or simply think of you.

I do this not so much to appease my own need to say this to you just once more, but rather to try and make up for all the times I inexcusably failed to say it before.

Westlawn Cemetery
Just wrapping up another visit with my Dad.

A Prayerful Thought

I dream and pray that on that solemn day when my sons pause to think of me, the one thing they're sure to see is a Dad who truly loves them with all his heart, and that they sleep well each night knowing my passing won't ever serve to keep us apart.

June 1, 2012
Fort Worth, TX
May my sons always remember just how much I love them.
By the way ... I officially retired today!

The only thing I take more comfort in than the memories I have of my Dad and our ongoing talks is in praying that one day we'll be together again, but this time it'll be forevermore!

July 4, 2012
Amarillo, TX
Celebrating my grandson Gabe's 9th birthday serves to
remind me that he's not the only one getting older!

I have no one to blame but myself for not spending more of my Dad's yesterdays with him, for he has no more tomorrows, to which I would give anything for but one.

Life After Death

A crazy thought just crossed my mind, although, as you've already read, that's not all that particularly unusual. With it being the love of my life's birthday, my Dad posed the following query for me to consider.

In the life after death, does one stay the same age they were when they passed, or do they continue getting older?

Now don't laugh! I actually want you to think about this and its consequences. I'm being totally serious ... really!

If our spouse passes on long before we do, and in the afterlife they don't age, we might be thirty years, or more, their senior by the time we join them, and that's praying we get to where they are!

So, here are my main concerns:

first, will I end up where I'm confident she'll be...

then, will she have gotten tired of waiting on me...

and finally, if I'm the only one to have aged, will she still be attracted to me, or will she simply then become nothing more than my perpetual and eternal caretaker?

Oh, and by all means, please, God, if you would ... don't let her forget how to cook!

August 3, 2012
I can only thank my Dad for spawning such entertaining thoughts.
PS to Pat: My Dad said to wish you a very Happy Birthday!

Remorse and Closure

At first, you might find this to be a bit of a stretch, but remorse and closure are two intimately related emotions we reluctantly leave behind.

Each time a true love one is lost a heavy dose of remorse gets passed down to their surviving love ones, with the warm embrace of closure standing far off in the distance.

It's only now that I've come to see that remorse will continue to taunt my aching heart as closure patiently waits for my ever-encroaching time to depart.

And it'll only be then when remorse and closure finally come to an end, for not until one is gone does one get to sadly pass it on.

New Orleans, LA ~ Airport
As I travel, so do my thoughts,
fears, and desires.

Closure and Remorse

With the passing of a love one, neither closure nor remorse comes through a conscious effort or purposeful thought. Instead, they silently and cautiously sneak up on us, slowly confronting and taunting our broken hearts.

If you haven't already, you too will eventually come to see how both closure and remorse are just as painful as they are elusive and will quickly become all-consuming.

I'm sure He has His reasons, but God only grants us relief from this emotional duo but once in a lifetime, for not until we too pass on will we get to finally embrace some long overdue peace of mind.

Houston, TX ~ Airport
With as many years as have come to pass,
closure and remorse still haunt me.

Are we not the caretakers of each heart we touch?

Mothe's Funeral Home
I'm just paying my respects to a truly good old friend.
Thoughtful listeners are clearly so much more
important and rare than are good talkers.

At Rest

It's taken me this many years to finally realize just how futile it is to try and emotionally set aside the agonizing thought of having lost a love one, even if we believe it to be only temporarily.

For not until long after they've been laid to rest will it become obvious that they are the only ones who will forever truly be at rest.

Amarillo, TX
An odd thought while spending some precious time with my grandkids.

I've come to see that changes to one's heart affect how they feel day to day and those within their soul may alter how they are yet to act, but changes to their spirit will forever transform the true essence of their entire being.

September 21, 2012
While celebrating my Mom's 87th birthday, when she went to blow out
the candles I had no doubt as to what she was wishing for.
My Dad's passing has clearly changed the
very core of her existence.

A brief intro for what's to follow...

Just a few minutes ago, as I was trying to compose some random thoughts into more meaningful words, I glanced up at a picture of my Dad, as I often do. If I'm perplexed or confounded, his reassuring smile always sets my creativity wheels into motion and in the direction which I need to go.

At that very moment, my attention was redirected to a song playing on the radio, to which the first line I heard was "till death do us part."

Having just looked at my Dad's picture and knowing how he so often speaks to me through others, I knew this was not just a mere coincidence.

The next thing I knew, I was frantically trying to capture every word I could feel being dictated to me. It was only after I finished jotting down what's to follow could I go back and read what I had just written.

Till Death Do Us Part

I understand "for richer or poorer, in sickness and in good health, and forsaking all others" being included in the marriage vows, for they suitably apply to two souls entering into an everlasting commitment to each other.

Correct me if I'm wrong, but is not the joining of two people in holy matrimony one of the utmost religious of all ceremonies? If so, then please tell me why "till death do us part" is also included in those beloved proceedings?

Was this simply inserted so we could get remarried, with the church's blessings, after a spouse dies? Yet, in the scriptures and teachings of virtually all religions, repeated reference is made to all of God's creatures being reunited, living happily ever after, in the hereafter. Then, if that's so, let's examine just a few of the challenging situations this could cause to arise.

Like here on earth, once one reaches Heaven, can they then move on to another partner while waiting for their first spouse to re-join them? I mean, they did make the "forsaking all others" commitment, did they not? And if they do move on, what happens if or when everybody gets there? Now I'm talking about everybody ... all the ex-wives and ex-husbands! In the hereafter, is it going to be just one big, happy family with all that's gone by being forgotten and forgiven? Clearly, no one knows this, but from what and who I do know, I truly don't think this will be so, but then again, we're talking about being in Heaven.

So, if we believe these almighty principles to be true, as well as there being a Heaven and hereafter, why do we openly accept and faithfully observe the possibility of such conflicting beliefs?

(Continued)

Though death is the ultimate finale, is it actually the only occasion by which we're allowed to get around what God has preordained to be a once and forever commitment to each other? Or, is it simply that the hereafter, and forever after, no longer restrict us as to what we do in the thereafter?

September 22, 2012
An especially creative and thoughtful gift from
my Dad on yet another of my birthdays!

So, does forever really have to last for ... ever?

Just as I've attempted to do in much of what I've already written, the purpose of my above entry is to likewise have you think of commonly accepted things a little bit differently than before, or at least from here on.

Clearly, changing one's thinking requires changing a lot more than just one's thoughts. For each word that's already been defined by another opens the door for it to be reinterpreted by others.

So, the next time you hear "till death do us part" think back to my views on this, and maybe you too will quietly begin to question some of the same things as do I.

And I thank you, Dad, for using humor to prompt us to reconsider what was once thought to mean but one thing.

When our heart aches, we hurt all over.
November 22, 2012
Because I miss my Dad so much, his absence reminds me
just how fortunate I am to still have my Mom.
Happy Thanksgiving, Dad.

Time has taught me how to deal with and reflect upon my Dad's absence. Although the more it passes, the more I learn not so much what I didn't know, but rather what I mistakenly thought I knew, but clearly didn't.

December 25, 2012
Holidays are a time for reflection and to appreciate what we have,
as well as what we've lost! Merry Christmas, Dad!

So
Many people would be so much happier if they didn't spend so much time seeking out so many ways to make themselves feel so damn miserable ... so often!

I know this because I was one of those so-so people myself.

As I touched on earlier, closure is one of the few words that unmistakably defines an emotion that's uniquely human, or so we're led to believe.

Usually, most of us choose to either avoid or refuse to consider the finality of losing a love one until we feel the time is right. I'm sorry to say this, but there will never come such a time.

By definition, closure doesn't extend a temporary reprieve to what our hearts refuse to believe; rather it's but a tiny part of a solution to a much larger problem that can never really be fixed, only briefly set aside.

One would think that once we embrace closure we can then move on, but sadly, not until we too pass on will we ever get to know and experience the true pleasure closure bestows upon an aching heart.

January 12, 2013
Carriere, MS
Learning to live with the loss of love ones is not nearly the same as living without them, and yes, Dad ... Happy Birthday!

How can one begin to believe what their heart is not yet ready to painfully concede?

As a military dad, I can't bear to watch other parents' anguish over the loss of a fallen love one and can only pray I'm not made to suffer the same. I'm so sorry for the loss they will forever be made to bear.

Words are miserably inadequate when it comes to thanking them for their service and collective sacrifices.

I now see that it's much wiser to simply ask questions in seeking the truth, rather than hide in the shadows of uncertainty or live in fear of what the truth might reveal.

I just wish I had asked my Dad so much more ... and more often.

4:32 AM

I had a dream last night that I just can't stop thinking about. With it feeling so real and being unable to go back to sleep, I felt the time it awoke me as a befitting title. I realized immediately that if I didn't get up and go capture what I still remembered; it would become yet another fragmented memory. So, here's all that I could recall:

Well, I was visiting with my Dad when this guy came up from out of nowhere. At first, I took him to be a cemetery worker, but that quickly changed. He stopped right next to me and began to read aloud a poem my Dad had written which we had inscribed onto a plaque attached to his headstone. Eventually, he quieted down and read the rest of it softly to himself. He then bowed his head and quietly uttered, "You come here pretty often, don't you? I've come to know your Dad really well; he's quite a man. It's easy to see why you miss him so much."

To say I was dumbstruck doesn't begin to explain how I felt. I remember looking at him and not being able to utter a word. He continued by saying, "He was one of the best 'fixers' I've ever known. There wasn't anything your Dad couldn't only fix but make it much better than it ever was."

At that point all I could do was to give him a big, broad grin and nod in agreement. To this he blurted out, "What the hell are you laughin' at? You ain't no different than him! Believe me, he's glad and proud to see that you're pickin' up right where he left off."

While trying to process all of this, I must have thanked him, as he replied, "That's okay; I'm not telling you anything he wouldn't want me to say. Your Dad breathed life into things that others regarded as being all but lost. It takes a very special person to fix special things." As I began to say "Yeah, but" he interrupted me with, "Well, I gotta' go. See ya' later," and walked away. I again found myself at a loss for words and could only say, "Thank you ... take care." I remember thinking to myself, no, don't wake up ... not yet!

What this gentleman said struck me to the core and has since stayed with me. To have someone compare me to my Dad is more than I could pray to hear, even if but in a dream. Although others have made somewhat similar comments, none has had such a lasting, heart-warming impact as did the words from this old, mythical soul.

(Continued)

To add to the uniqueness of this experience, my newly found friend managed to fulfill a special wish I had expressed to my Dad a long time ago and continue to pray for each night.

If you'll recall, in a much earlier entry, "A Private Message to My Dad," I wrote, in part, "Until that day when we're reunited forevermore ... please talk to me in my dreams..." Well, this is exactly what he was doing, even if but through an unknown entity.

With the loss of my Dad, I learned quickly that I couldn't fix everything or breathe life back into the most precious of all my wants. I've accepted that last night was just another example of him doing what he has always done best. He knew my heart was hurting and in bad need of repair, so once again as I've come to depend, he finds a way to let me know he'll always be right there.

Each night, I now look forward to dreaming, for I view
them as special times, never to be wasted.

Remaining quiet because your heart can't find just the right things to say is not only hard but sometimes leaves you with more than just your words left unsaid.

Reflecting on the problems I sometimes have
in trying to talk with my Mom.

Fifteen years ago, and the only thing reality that little to does it seem likely it **15 Years** almost to the minute, that's changed is the nothing has ... nor ever will!

April 14, 2013
Seldom am I at such a loss for words. Sure, I could find more to say,
but I still wouldn't be saying what needs to be said.

As hard as it is to always do the right thing, our conscience has a way of making it even harder to live with knowing we willfully did something wrong.

Yet, to carry that premise a step further, this would require all of us to have a conscience, but then ... do we?

And it's just as frustrating as it's impossible to try and
make things right once you no longer can.

Some Thoughts on Emotions

Clearly, without emotions there would be no feelings, and without feelings, what else would there be a need for? Virtually everything we do, say, seek, deny, or affirm can, in some way, be tied to an emotion. If you disagree, I challenge you to name something, anything, meaningful that doesn't involve an emotion. Now, in trying to do so, be careful that your emotions don't lead you down a pointless path, for they are rather shrewd and calculating.

Emotions are quite perplexing. They'll excite and elevate you to new heights; then, in the very next minute, they'll deeply and ruthlessly entomb you. Oddly, it only takes but the very slightest of differences in circumstances for any one given emotion to either entice one's wildest, undisclosed desires or subdue another's unresolved rage.

Images evoked by emotions help us to remember irreplaceable moments in time long since thought of as forgotten, while painfully resurrecting memories we truly wish we could no longer recall.

And for those rare instances that occur but a few times in one's life, it's not the details of what happened, but moreover the emotions attached to these events that are forever etched into our hearts and minds. Emotions don't really ever change; it's just that our hearts have learned to swap one for another to better fit the moment.

Without emotions, would life truly be worth living? Think about this ... really! To describe true love without the emotion that defines it would be like attempting to express true hatred minus the fury that feeds it. Then, is it even possible to explain the pain of losing a love one, or even a close friend, absent the numbing emotions that cloud the very words you struggle to speak?

Many words would have no meaning if it were not for the emotions that spurred them into being. And there would be no moral compass to guide us, if not for the emotions that quietly protect and insulate us.

So, what basis would there be to rejoice today, or even mourn tomorrow, without the emotions that serve to motivate either over whelming joy or endless sorrow?

July 4, 2013
Amarillo, TX
I don't only thank God for giving us emotions, but moreover,
for the ability to not just feel but share them as well.
Happy 10th Birthday to our first grandchild, Gabe.

Okay … One More

Every emotion has a flavor of its own; be it bitter or sweet, they nonetheless tease and torment the palate of one's heart and serve to satisfy both the boldest and most demure amongst us.

September 21, 2013
Sorry, sometimes my emotions get both the better and the bitter of me!
Happy Birthday, Mom.

Sixty-Two

Well, I finally and thankfully managed to hit sixty-two! With that said, I'm having trouble remembering where I was when sixty-one came to pass, though, as you've read, my fiftieth was one I'll never forget.

If you'll look back you'll see that I've spent entirely too many of my birthdays all alone and too far from home; however, today that happily changed. I was finally fortunate enough to be able to share it with the love of my life, and once again, four very dear friends.

While I enjoyed more than my share of cake and excellent wine, one of my cohorts made a passing comment that I'll never forget and meant more to me than any gift I could have ever received. She said that with reading as much of this book as her heart would permit, knowing me as well as she does, and considering all that she's heard about my Dad, she come to see a lot of him in me.

At that point, my sixty-second birthday was complete and better than anything I could have prayed for, regardless of whatever else we might do. Being earnestly compared to my Dad wasn't just a gift, but a God-sent answer to a lifelong prayer.

This entry is my way of thanking these friends for making this milestone one to remember. In particular, I'd like to let my friend, Beckie, know that by what she said gave me something I'll truly cherish forever.

September 22, 2013
Carriere, MS
Thanks to my lovely wife and friends, for seeing to it that this was a
very special 62nd birthday. And to Beckie, once again, I bid
you an extra special thanks for your kind words.

Some

There are some words that need absolutely no help from others to express exactly what they were meant to proclaim, for their clarity allows them to boldly stand alone on their own merit.

Yet, there are some words like day, where, how, and time which have little meaning when spoken all by themselves. Then, if you simply add the word "some" to the front of each, they take on an entirely new and profound meaning.

Someday, somewhere, and somehow, we'll all be together again; and thanks to God ... for quite some time.

October 25, 2013
Lancaster, PA
This came about while describing my Dad to his great-grandson Logan, following his 5th birthday party!

Tiny Droplets

By now, you may have come to expect, and I hope kindly accept, my drawing together some unassociated thoughts in odd and equally unconventional ways. With that disclaimer, I'll ask you to bear with me as I capture yet another unusual vision that just occurred to me.

Each time I write an entry that I too must reread to fully absorb the message it contains, I'm often amazed as to how those very words actually arise. I've since come to happily accept that they are remnants of the many messages my Dad had left unsaid, which he's now passing on through me.

Since I still cannot imagine such verses as coming from my pen alone, in my mind, I sought a plausible way to explain how all this comes about.

It was then when the following vision came to me: All the words my Dad had yet to say were randomly stuffed deeply into the bowels of my pen as but tiny droplets of ink. And there they stay, patiently waiting for him to help guide me while I roll them out and he carefully rearranges them upon each new page.

December 24, 2013
This thought came to me while I was trying to think of something special to write on my Mom's Christmas card.

Happy New Year ... I Guess?

Sorry, Dad; but as you know, I intended to visit with you before it became too late, but I got hung up trying to get Mom to eat dinner. So, if you would, please bear with me while I vent just a little.

Well, I don't think I need to tell you how Mom's health and mental state have been declining, and of the many problems that this is causing for her. Believe me, I know you're trying to help, as she keeps telling us just how much she sees and talks with you. And in that regard, with no disrespect intended, I truly envy her.

However, as you are also aware, there are some very worrisome and difficult decisions I'll soon need to make regarding Mom's future well-being. I say I'm the one needing to make these choices, but Pat, Denny, and Syl are actively and equally involved with what is likely to soon take place. Though they are all in agreement, with me being here with Mom, day in and day out, I often feel isolated and too much in control of something I can't and truly wish need not be controlled.

Though I've been trying to prepare both her and myself for what lies ahead, Mom doesn't seem to grasp the reality any better than I've come to terms with the gravity of it all. I guess in her case that might be a good thing. Life with Mom has taught me that it's best not to tell her what she can no longer understand, and clearly doesn't want to hear. My greatest fear is that what I must do will cause her to question and begin to doubt my love for her.

All I ask of you is to help us get through this, and if you would, the next time you visit with her, please, in spite of what's to come, let her know just how much I now and will always love her.

January 1, 2014
Some paths we must travel are very dark, regardless of the time of day.

The pain one suffers from the loss of a love one can only be partially shared with another. However, it can be made more tolerable by allowing those closest to us to bear that which they lovingly choose to help us carry.

In this regard, I pray you are as fortunate as am I.

Believe me, I truly hesitate to say or even think this, but I really wish I wasn't going home to what I fear I'm going home to.

Oh, how I wish there were something ... anything, I could do to help my Mom feel better.

January 12, 2014
Carriere, MS
Happy Birthday, Dad!

I've heard it said on any number of occasions and under a variety of different types of circumstances that simply ... "Life is what it is."

Though brief, these few words are collectively quite profound, and unassumingly insightful, but if anything, they're not simple.

I'm here to tell you that far too often "Life is ... just what it is" in spite of all my continuing heartfelt prayers to the contrary!

If this confuses you, don't worry; so was I when I wrote it.

To Say

When the moment requires you say nothing, that doesn't mean you have nothing to say; it may just not be the right time to say it.

And there are so many times when you feel you should say something, but you just can't seem to find the right words to say.

February 13, 2014
Before meeting with representatives of Our Lady of Wisdom Nursing Facility,
I stopped by to see Mom. When I walked in, she was smiling like seldom
before, so I asked her why was she so happy? She quickly said,
"Oh, nothing, I'm just waiting for Ferdy to get back home."
I told her, "Yep ... That'll make me happy too!"

So, Dad ... What Do I Do?

With Mom's health and ability to remain home alone diminishing more and more, I can no longer escape from what's now become unavoidable. I truly wish I weren't faced with a choice I prayed never to make and going back on a promise to you I swore never to break. Would it do any good if I were to pray harder, and if so, please tell me ... just how do I do that?

Either you or God Himself had to have sent us the angel that we hired to take care of Mom for the past year or so. Living alone for so very long, it's taken her quite a while to adapt to having someone with her most of the day. Having said that, I hope she doesn't ask her to leave again, which she did yesterday, and the day before, and I've lost track of how many times before that. I guess we'll just wait to see what tomorrow brings.

So, what I'm seeking is your guidance as to whether or not what we've decided is the right thing for Mom. Her sitter is there from dawn to dusk, with Pat and me being there evenings, holidays, and weekends. However, her increasing physical inabilities are making this routine dangerously inadequate. What I'm really concerned about is her well-being each night when she's left all alone, albeit in the safety of her own home.

As you know, when I've stayed with Mom, she's really never at peace; repeatedly insisting that I go home, that I didn't need to stay, and only stopped saying so once she fell asleep. And please don't think badly of me, but neither she nor I can continue to live this way. Simply having no choice over doing what I must now do doesn't release me from the guilt that's to follow, nor will it ever make doing so any easier.

I realize this is asking a lot, but I'd appreciate it if you'd find a way to let me know that Mom's going to be okay, and I'm doing right by her. Having been her caretaker for so long, I feel like I'm abandoning her. And yes, I realize everyone agrees we have no other choice, but believe me, that's of little consequence, for what truly concerns me is will Mom understand that as well?

March 18, 2014
Earlier today, we finalized arrangements with Our Lady of Wisdom on my Mom's behalf.
This evening, after scribbling down what's above, I could see where my Dad used my
own words to help convince me of what I needed to hear and begin to accept.

Times

Though my Dad and I spoke heart to heart more often than I did with my Mom, the mutual suffering we've shared since his passing has brought us together like nothing else has ever before.

While recalling some of the good times, Mom and I often laughed till we cried. And likewise, we cried even more when thinking back over some of the times that maybe weren't all that good. But, what's more important than all of this is that at no time did anything ever cause us to question or doubt our love for each other ... absolutely never! What I'm afraid of is that what's soon to happen may cause all of that to change.

I can only pray that when it finally comes down to it, in the recesses of my Mom's mind, she'll remember my love for her, and that it is my unwavering devotion that's forcing me to do the very thing that may cause her to begin questioning everything.

I don't see how it will ever be possible for me to sincerely convince
myself of something my heart is has yet even begun to accept?

There are very few nights in which I don't weep over memories I wish not to keep. Then, if that weren't bad enough, I often lie awake praying for God's sake, He keep my love ones from making my same mistakes.

My, oh my ... to only now know all that I would,
could, or should have done so differently.

Which Will It Be?

With me and my Dad always having Mom on our minds, the two of us joust to see who can recall what stands out as the best of our happier times. More often than not, our talks always wander back to her younger days, when she cleverly used her conniving and wily ways, to somehow get away with doing things others wouldn't even think to do, but again, that was our dear Shirley ... tried and true.

Above all else, her unwavering love and devotion to family and friends is what gives rise to many of our talks and continues to fondly inspire our yet to be written words and thoughts.

(Continued)

Then, in spite of all our prayers, too often life takes us in a direction that's neither of our choosing nor under our control. And if you've been a student of how I've outlined the narrowing path my Mom is now traveling, you'll know my feelings and fears on that; but again, and sadly, her life continues to unfold.

On the one hand, I'm slowly losing my Mom with each day that passes. She's drifting further and further away, right in front of me, and I don't know how to stop it. But, the one thing I do know is that her health is no longer in question; rather, it's now at risk.

What's equally as bad is that she's slowly losing me just as well, and just as surely. With dementia there are times when she knows not who I am. My concern is which is going to be worse: will her not grasping any of what's to happen be a hidden blessing, or will my not telling her the full truth turn into a never-ending curse?

Because Mom has so few days left that she'll spend in her house,
rather, her home, I don't know how or if I should try to
make today any different or better, that's even if
I could, which I don't think I can.

A Clear Sign

I'm sorry, but I can't get it off my mind that in just a few days I'll be doing something I promised you I would never, ever do. And though Mom may not have heard me speak the very words I so often swore to you, I still meant them just the same, praying that by speaking softly I'd shield her from such pain. So, now, instead of just one promise, I'm sadly breaking two.

Although I've tried everything I thought was even remotely possible to prevent this from happening, I failed again, and yes ... miserably. There's got to be something I didn't do that I could or should have, and if there is, please tell me what it might be!

Mom listens to you; she believes and trusts in you. So, please let her know that in spite of what she'll soon come to see, and likely think of me, I'd gladly swap places with her before the setting of this day's sun will have ever begun. I truly pray you don't have to, but if you do, please remind her again that I love her so, so very much.

(Continued)

You know how much I've worried and struggled over taking Mom out of her home, the site of her birth that gives her a sense of identity and vestige of self-worth. Yet, here I am trying to find something I can say when it comes time to take her away, to a place she's only visited a few times before, but now will likely stay forevermore.

Pat said something to me earlier that has caused me to start thinking quite differently about my role in what's getting ready to happen. In so many words she said that I'm looking at this as being something I'm doing to my Mom, rather than for her.

So, at this point in time, all I can ask for is some kind of sign, absolutely anything, to let me know if Pat is just as right as I feel I am wrong.

Our Lady of Wisdom
I just had to come here again to make sure that I'm
definitely sure about what I'm still so unsure of.

> *Though this next entry is longer than I had intended, it tells more than just one story and reveals something I truly wanted to keep to myself.*
>
> *I hope by sharing this you too will start watching for all those little tokens you previously walked right by, and come to cherish each of them as the treasured "signs" your love ones placed there with loving care just for you to find.*

Ask, and Ye Shall Receive

So, what does this have to do with me now divulging my little secret to you? Well, besides the many words my Dad and I have already shared, there's another clever way he came up with to stay in touch with me.

Because of how this first came about, and then evolved into such an unusual but ongoing way for us to stay connected, I chose to keep it to myself. I wanted it to remain just between him and me, which is why I've kept my words carefully concealed for no others to see.

However, in looking back at what he managed to pull off at not just his burial but ever since then, and yet again earlier today, there's absolutely no way I can stay silent about this any longer. For there are some things that simply must be shared with this being one of them.

Now, I need to take you back to the very day of my Dad's burial to fill you in on the story that forms the very basis behind this entire story … his first clear "sign."

(Continued)

When it came time to leave the cemetery, I stayed close by my Mom to help comfort her. On our way to the limo she paused to look back at Dad, and then gazed up at me. I'll never forget the sheer sense of loss and emptiness I saw in her eyes with the essence of her entire being draining away with each step we took. Once I got her into the limo, I too looked back to bid my Dad yet another, but certainly not a final goodbye. What happened next forever changed how I believe and will ever after view the ongoing presence of our love one's lingering spirit. Once again, my Dad came through in a way that surprised even me.

As I turned back around, my attention wasn't just drawn away; it felt more like it was being forcibly redirected to, of all things, a penny lying on the ground in amongst a pile of pine needles; that's right ... a mere penny lying there so innocently and unnoticeably. I remember pausing and thinking with where I am, and considering all that was taking place, why is this tiny, irrelevant object distracting me so and demanding my sole, undivided attention? How can that be, and why is this now happening to me?

Well, I really don't remember picking it up, but I do recall feeling that if I didn't, I would truly come to regret it. With Mom being my main and only concern, I never gave my copper comrade a second thought, at least not for a while.

It wasn't until later, when I was at my Mom's changing clothes, that I came across my little metallic friend once again. Actually, I had forgotten that I even had it. While emptying my pockets, when I touched it that same sense of wonder, and of my being so closely attached to it, washed over me. And even though a lot of people were still there, it became eerily silent as I held it, examined it, and thought back to how curiously it came to be. Then why, at such a mournful place and time, did it reveal itself to just me? That was when I realized it had to have been my Dad's way of giving me a unique and clear sign that he intends to keep in touch by leaving small tokens for me to hereafter find.

Knowing how my Dad tends to do things, when I looked a lot more closely at my tiny tarnished friend, I wasn't surprised to find it dated 1998. Now that's not the year before, two, three, or maybe even more; rather, it's from that very year, the year of his passing. And if you believe this to be a sheer coincidence, then I suggest you read on.

(Continued)

With all of this as background, I now must ask you to flash forward to the day on which what's to follow will bring everything into perspective. I caution you, as you continue, to keep in mind this tiny, yet all-important sign.

As I toil over my Mom's worsening situation, it saddens me that I can only watch as her clock of independence slowly but methodically ticks down. But, if I could just go talk with my Dad before the sun sets later today, he would let me know if what I must now do is truly the right way.

Yet, all the while driving to the cemetery, I couldn't stop questioning all the choices I both had and didn't have. Is what I'm about to do for Mom right or wrong, and will he answer my plea? Then, what do I do if he somehow shows me to be wrong, or worse yet, doesn't even answer me?

By this time, to say I was upset fails dreadfully short at explaining how worried I truly was when I drove up and finally parked. But, unlike any of our many other visits, this time I had a vague, unsure feeling that I might not find what I went there seeking. As I walked toward where my Dad lay resting, a totally foreign, unusually cold, and eerily unwelcomed presence seemed to hover about and angrily intervene, increasing my already nervous uncertainty.

It was then when I heard what could only have been the devil whispering in my ear, "I'll see to it you don't find that all-important sign, and when you leave, I'll make sure you wish you'd never even come here." Needless to say, all I could do was to think to myself, what if that's true? What if I don't find so much as a single sign, then what am I to do? The more steps I took, the more frantically I looked, in every crack and cranny. Please, God, if You would, and Dad, if you could; all I'm asking for is a simple sign in the form of but another mere penny.

As I approached my Dad, I anxiously bowed my head so he and I could talk. Though from here on most of my words will be directed just to him, because of what he did and ends up revealing, I really think you just might want to continue listening in.

By the time I stood before my Dad, there was no sign to be had. So, I thought, why did you choose this, of all times, to not give me at least some kind of a sign? But then, if you provide me with none, am I to take the absence of one as being the very sign I was angrily told just minutes ago I wasn't going to find?

(Continued)

You, more than anyone, know that I came here looking for neither pity nor absolution, but a message that's clear and true; one that lets me know what I'm doing for Mom is the very same she would expect of you. But yet, as I tried to say before, I'm actually praying and hoping for a little something more.

Well, never in my wildest dreams, most solemn prayers, or highest of hopes would I ever have imagined that you could do what you did today. I also can't believe how you were able to again use the same simplest of signs to ease my mind and alleviate all the concerns I'm now struggling over with Mom.

The next thing I knew, just as with that first penny following your burial, once again you forced my attention to a place I would likely not have looked. Lying there, perched on the top ledge of your tombstone, was the sign I'd come there praying to find. In my heart I knew this was your special way of letting me know that what I'm doing for Mom is exactly what needs to be done. Then, the skeptical side of me began to come through; am I truly seeing what I think I'm seeing, and if so, am I to take this as a message from you?

Though in my heart I truly wanted to believe, with tear-filled eyes I leaned a little closer to get a more certain look. Yet, with all that's now weighing so heavily on my mind, it wasn't until I looked up again did I finally see what I came there to find. Knowing this day was coming, you clearly had to have placed it there quite some time ago. As you can see above, this old, rust-encrusted coin lay hidden behind a layer of dust and cobwebs, barely letting it show.

At first, I didn't want to touch or even disturb it as I stood there glaring and staring at it, totally in awe. Then, a fear came over me that if I looked away, would it stay, and did I really see what I thought I saw?

The one thing I knew was I couldn't leave without it, for more than anything else it let me know you agree that I'm doing the right thing for Mom. Once again, by revealing this critically important sign, you've managed to completely relieve my previously conflicted and worried mind.

Now, back to you, my friend, and the rest of the story.

(Continued)

I realize it took me a while to get you to this point, but it's a point we really needed to get to. I hope sharing these experiences and events helps you to get a much better and more complete understanding of the unique, ongoing relationship I pray to always have with my Dad.

To date, I can only show you the hundreds of physical signs I've found, or better said ... have found me. For by now you know that their true value lies not in their number, but in the fact that each represents, at least in my heart, a singular and distinctly personal message from my Dad.

March 24, 2014
Westlawn Cemetery
For revealing yourself to me, so often,   I love and thank you all the more.

An added note...

Who hasn't heard of pennies from heaven or stopped to pick up a coin that they've come across? Although it doesn't appear so, this chest measures 10 by 5 inches, and the basket is a little over 6 inches wide with both being about 5 inches deep. Together they currently hold a yet to be counted sample of every coin imaginable, even paper and foreign currency. Believe me, this represents just a portion of the more visible signs I've collected since my Dad's passing. Though the spiritual ones go unseen and can't be counted, they still count all the more. And you can rest assured ... they are kept just as safely stowed and closely guarded by my heart.

To my wife's dismay, I now go well out of my way to pick up each and every coin I come across, no matter where we are or who we're with. I never would have thought or ever imagined that something so simple as a coin lying in my path would come to mean and represent so very much: my Dad leaving a silent, yet clearly tangible message ... especially intended for me. For this and more, I love him so!

With all the words I've hoarded in my many inscribing years, I can find none, not even so much as one, that'll help me prepare Mom for what's yet to come.

March 26, 2014
Later today we'll be bringing my Mom to Our Lady of Wisdom. Without a doubt,
this is absolutely the second most difficult thing I will ever have done.

Dad, though I feel there's really no need to ask this of you, but with my level of uncertainty and concern being what it is, I can't help myself.

If you would, please be waiting at Our Lady of Wisdom to greet and comfort Mom ... and yes, me as well!

March 26, 2014
We're getting Mom ready, and thankfully, I guess, she just
thinks we're taking her for nothing but a little ride.

How Dare Me!

Though I tried again this morning to prepare my Mom for what was going to happen later today, she still didn't grasp what I was talking about. Then, once it came time to take her to the nursing facility, I felt many of the very same feelings and emotions as I did while driving to the funeral home to make my Dad's final arrangements. I knew I wasn't losing my Mom, but I still couldn't shake the feeling that the closeness I always had with her was likely to never be the same ever again.

Well, once we arrived and after making absolutely sure she was settled in and comfortable, though she had little to say, I couldn't stop talking. I now see where hidden in every word was my futile way of letting her know how sorry I was. So, I kissed her, told her I love her, and that I would return real soon.

As I glanced back, the faraway, empty look in her eyes told me she still didn't know where she was ... but I did. She could tell something wasn't quite right or knew what it was ... but I did. And she didn't understand that we alone would be leaving, but again ... I did. I can only pray that God didn't keep her waiting for me to return nearly as long as I did wishing that I had.

I'll never forget how hard it was to leave the cemetery the day we laid my Dad to rest. I remember feeling I was somehow abandoning him, but the finality of his passing left me with no choice. Although my Mom's situation is totally different, thank God, and even with my Dad having given me his sign of approval, I just know I'll forever regret and question my doing what I've done. If you'll recall, I wasn't with my Dad at his ultimate time of need. Now, here I am leaving my Mom when she needs me the most. How dare me!

(Continued)

Much later, after I got home, I sat down to capture my thoughts before they became too entangled to unravel. The first feeling to cross my mind, which I jotted down, was how it went better than I had prayed for or could have ever expected it to go. Yet, before I could place a period upon that very sentence my heart scorned and scolded me, sharply and deeply, as well it should. Better! Better than what? How dare me!

To even conceive such a self-serving thought, at such a difficult and trying time, not for me, but for my Mom. How it went today has absolutely nothing whatsoever to do with me, but her, and her alone. Dam it; how dare me!

In spite of all his efforts, this is the one time where even my Dad can't repair how the love of his life now sees their youngest son to be. All it took was that last look to let me know she's lost what faith she ever had in me.

Then, before I could delete the very words that so rightfully offended my confused heart, yet once again, my Dad intervened with an entirely different thought. I could feel him encouraging me to move beyond what my words first seemed to say, simply by asking me to consider, for Mom's sake, would I have really wanted it to go any other way?

March 26, 2014
Reality and emotions are best viewed through a different set of eyes.
Again, I can only thank my Dad for bringing some sense of
clarity to an otherwise very unclear moment in time.

One Day, and Counting

I visited with Mom today, actually twice; first to spend some time together, and then later to drop off some more clothes. The first time she was sleeping, but when she heard my voice she awoke. "Who's that … Ferdy?" "No, Mom, it's just me." "Oh, I thought it might'a been Ferdy. You know, you sound so much like him. He said he's coming back." "That's good. That's really good. I just pray I'm still here when he returns!" Quietly, she said, "Me too," and slid back into a deep, sound sleep.

March 27, 2014
Our Lady of Wisdom
I wish there was some way I could make her day
even half as good as she just made mine.

The time I spend mourning my Dad's passing is time that would be better spent enjoying that which I still have with my Mom.

Clearly, I need to learn how to cope with my feelings for my Dad so I can begin giving more of myself to my Mom.

One Week, and Counting

Well, a week has finally passed, and Mom keeps telling me how she likes all her nurses, and how sweet they are, but she wants to know why she hasn't seen a doctor yet.

Along with other things she's said, that tells me she thinks she's in a hospital. Then, when considering it, that may not be such a bad thing. So, Dad, because she believes whatever you say, if for nothing more than her peace of mind, please keep telling her that's right where she is.

April 2, 2014

Bittersweet Sixteen

There are things my Dad both had and did that truly fulfilled his life, and in **16** ways I can only pray to one day be blessed to have and do.

Of all that he had, the one thing I want and long for more than **Years** anything else is his close and truly loving relationship with all of his grandkids. For not only did he dearly love them, but he knew of their hearts' true. And if this weren't enough, I can tell they still love and long for his closeness each and every time they speak so lovingly and thoughtfully of him.

April 14, 2014
So, Dad, is there any way you can help ensure
that they feel the same for me?

Hopeful Thinking

I hope that, at least in God's eyes, my now being a much better, albeit older, wiser, and more contrite, adult will begin to make up for all the heartaches and torment I may have caused Him, my Dad, Mom, and so many others.

Here again, I'm praying the end result of my life's work will be enough for the good Lord to reunite me with my Dad.

And as you're soon to read ... with my Mom as well.

Silent Requests

The caring and devoted way in which my sons show their loving respect for their Paw-Paw and continually ask how their Maw-Maw is doing stands as proof positive that they're continually in their prayers, hearts, and thoughts.

I also see them doing things that my Dad had to have taught them and saying things that only my Mom would have said. With each action and word, whether they realize it or not, they are paying them a loving tribute that continues to please their souls and warm their hearts.

Though I still ask a lot of my Dad, if I could beg for just two additional things, I would feel a lot more at ease. I would first ask that when he's talking with God, he gets Him to help Mom feel happier and more contented. I'd also be forever blessed if He would have my sons and grandkids love and remember me just as much and in the same way as they do of him and my Mom.

Though keeping her safe, healthy, and comfortable, and knowing that she'll eventually be reunited with my Dad top my bucket list, I must admit that how my love ones forever feel for and think of me runs a real close second.

April 18, 2014
Amarillo, TX
*I pray the good Lord helps me do the same for my children and for theirs
as well, two of whose birthdays we're celebrating today.*
Happy Birthday to Hunter and Hailee.

I now see how and why my Dad saw himself to be the least important of all that he loved and cherished. I can say this because of the countless times I saw him put others first and well ahead of his own personal needs.

By remaining a step or so behind, he made sure he was always in place to catch us if we ever stumbled. I feel I've faltered with my Mom in a way that even my Dad can't fix

Once again, I'm second-guessing if what I'm doing for my Mom is right.

Though guilt is as strong of an emotion as is the sorrow it breeds, it's nowhere near as healing, or lasting, as will be the gift of forgiveness we sinners pray to someday receive.

June 1, 2014
Carriere, MS
Celebrating two years of my retirement with some dear friends.

Be Careful What You Ask For

Clearly, it's unsettling having to wait to be reunited with our departed love ones. However, I don't recall ever hearing my Dad say or even indicate a desire to return, if he could, once he had departed. Though this never really came up, this thought began to oddly somewhat bother me.

As badly as I want to see and embrace him again, I guess I naïvely believed that if God were to allow him to return, He surely wouldn't let him come back as sick and frail as he was when He took him. What purpose would that serve?

I now see where my own selfishness clouded not just what was possible but what I might actually be praying for. Clearly, I'm not seeking what I wanted without regard to what my Dad might have to contend with if he did return. Yet, again, let there be no doubt; I want him back, and with all my heart, but not at the cost of what this might impose upon him.

Too often we ask or even pray for things without regard to what it might require of another. So, just how would we feel if the tables were turned?

Well, rather than see my Dad return in such discomfort and pain, I sometimes wonder if it might just be best if I went to him? I suppose my aching heart will simply have to wait and bear his absence until the day comes when God decrees for that to happen.

Bedford, TX
To which I can only pray I end up going to where I know he is.

There Still Is

Sometimes I feel I have little love left to give. I wish it weren't so, but my Dad's departure has sadly affected a large part of my heart which remains.

And although such emptiness and voids in our lives are difficult to fill, just having my wife, sons, or grandkids simply hug me, or to see my Mom smile and especially laugh good-heartedly, quickly reminds me that there's still so very much to be thankful for.

I guess I just need to keep reminding myself that life will forever be worth living as long as I have someone who truly loves me and I'm able to return the same onto them.

Our Lady of Wisdom
God bless their patience, tolerance, and understanding.

Happy Birthday, Mom

With Mom turning eighty-nine today, Pat and I threw her a birthday party. Her new friends and all her nurses came and sang "Happy Birthday," and wished her well while sharing some of her favorite cake and ice cream. The old Shirley we know so well thanked each of them for coming, made sure they all had enough to eat and drink, and even ate more than usual herself.

As the party wound down, I could tell she was getting tired, so we took her back to her room. After helping her to get comfortable, we talked over old times, and even had a laugh or two. Then, as I was letting her know we would be leaving, she asked, "Gary ... Can you go find out if they got my test results back yet, and if I can go home today?"

Well, once again, I reluctantly struggled to tell her I would go find out what I could, but clearly my response was a lot less convincing than I thought. Sensing that, she released me from my torment by simply saying, "That's okay; I'll just get Ferdy to go talk to 'em. I think I'm gonna take a nap. I love you." All I could think to say was "Yes, Mom, if anyone can find out something from them it'll be Daddy ... and I love you too."

September 21, 2014
Our Lady of Wisdom
I could tell Mom was happy to have Dad at her party, but she would have been a lot happier if she could have left with him ... or even us.

Every time I visit with Mom, even before I get out of the car, I'm trying to think of what to say when she asks what I already know she's going to. Then, each time I walk into her room, if she's awake, I can tell by the look in her eyes that she's hoping today's the day I've come to take her home. Yet, knowing I'm not makes my first words to her harder, if that's even possible, than the last ones I speak before I leave.

Dad, I know you see and understand my predicament, but there's got to be some way you can get Mom to better understand hers as well. I'm at a loss as to what else I can say or do. So, if you would, please help Mom ... and me too.

September 21, 2014
Westlawn Cemetery
After leaving my Mom, I visited my Dad hoping to get some solutions to questions I fear won't aren't likely have any good answers.

A Very Special Visitor

Earlier today, while I was doing some writing and editing, I was distracted by a small moth that flew down right in front of me. Then, after being gone for a minute or two, it came back and darted around aimlessly. Although I was focused on what I was doing, it didn't take long for it to become a real disruption. Just as I decided to rid myself of this little intruder, it flew off to somewhere behind me. Honestly, I was somewhat put at ease to see it fly away.

Quite often while I'm writing, I pause to look up at a picture of my Dad for support and inspiration. As I looked back and glanced up, I could see my petite airborne prowler had returned. It wasn't just flying around like before. Instead, it zipped back and forth directly in front of my computer screen, just as if it was truly trying to get my attention.

With it becoming a real annoyance, I quickly reached up to catch and rid myself of its presence. After a few tries, I finally managed to grab it. I then squeezed my hand tightly closed and slowly opened it. I expected to see it lying there squashed and lifeless, but to my utter surprise, it was virtually unharmed.

Then, to my dismay, it immediately flew up directly toward my Dad's picture. Needless to say, my little friend not only had my full and undivided attention, I could do nothing but intently watch as it freely skirted back and forth. However, it now seemed almost invigorated and no longer afraid as it knew it need not fear me anymore.

It was in those few moments when I realized there was something really special about my tiny winged comrade. As much as I wanted it to, could it be my Dad's way of letting me know he was right there with me? By that time the only sound that could be heard, other than the beating of my heart, was the soft fluttering of my little friend's wings.

A few seconds later it flew down directly in front of me, again, just as if it knew it was safe to do so. This time it didn't fly back and forth; instead, it flew as if it had both direction and a purpose. To my surprise it landed on a stack of pages I had just finished printing and calmly sat there slowly raising and lowering its wings as if to be resting.

(Continued)

I then gently placed my finger right in front of it to see what it would do. Instead of flying away, like I had thought it would, it leisurely crawled up onto my finger, and even slower yet, into the palm of my hand.

I immediately grabbed my phone and took the picture that's inset on the previous page. Because I was afraid it might fly away, I made sure I had a good, clear snapshot before I went inside to show it to Pat. While I explained what all had just occurred, we watched as it continued to quietly sit comfortably in my hand, still slowly lowering and raising its wings. I knew the only thing left to do was to bring it outside and set it free, just like I'm sure my Dad is now happy to be.

As I held out my fully opened hand, it sat there and continued to gently flutter its wings. To say it was waving goodbye would be a stretch, but after what had happened minutes ago ... who am I to say? It then flew straight up and away, knowing it had accomplished exactly what it came there to do. I must admit that although a part of me was sorry for it to leave, I was equally pleased to know it's now able to travel wherever it desires. And yes, each time I look up at my Dad's picture, I hope my tiny friend returns.

When I went back to my office, my words seemed to take on a new meaning, and even if only to me had more importance than before. By now, you know my Dad is my main driving force, but I see this visit as proof-positive that we are so much more than just pen pals.

Needless to say, from that day forth, any creatures that now make their way into my office are welcome to stay and visit for just as long as they wish.

September 22, 2014
Another surprise visit from my Dad making this yet another extra special birthday!

I can now only wish I would have helped my Mom do and enjoy some of the things on her bucket list, but sadly she's never shared them with me.

What bothers me even more is that I never took the time to ask her what they might be.

October 25, 2014
China Springs, TX
Well, I'm trying my best to make some of my grandson Logan's
bucket list come true. Happy Birthday, Mr. Man!

Please dear Lord, give me the compassion, ability, and power to soothe another's grief-stricken heart as so many did to mine; even if the difference I'm able to make is of the tiniest amount. For how often, is it not, the littlest of things that truly matter the most at such mournful times.

Carriere, MS
While in a grocery store, I overheard someone telling a friend of their recent loss.
You have no idea how bad I wanted to give them the hug they so badly needed.

A Meaningful Encounter

The other day, following a visit with my Dad, I ended up walking along side of an elderly lady who also happened to be leaving. When we got to the parking area she asked me, "Do you come here very often?" I told her, "Well, as much as I can." Then, with a distinctly different tone she replied, "So, when we leave if the better part of us stays behind, I guess we really never leave ... do we?" Not expecting that, I found myself saying, "No, I don't suppose we ever do. Thank you! Really ... thank you for that thought."

She continued, but this time with an odd but pleasing look in her eyes; the kind that only comes with age and a life well lived. "You know, he was right; you are a good boy!" I guess my puzzled look led her to then say, "Oh, you mean you didn't hear him?" Before I could say a word, she smiled, got into her car, and smiled again as she slowly drove away.

Since that encounter, every time I visit with my Dad, I no longer feel so bad when it comes time to leave because I now know I never really do with the better part of me remaining behind.

This odd discussion caused me to rethink the dream I captured and entitled "4:32 am."
Her demeanor conveyed the very same feelings as did the gentleman in that entry
and leads me to wonder if he might have been her departed husband?

When you begin to struggle over what more can be done for an ailing love one, know that simply talking to and spending more time with them is the best thing you'll ever hope to do for them, and in the long run ... yourself as well.

November 27, 2014
Dumas, TX
Since my brother came in to spend some time with Mom, and not having seen our son,
Craig, his wife Christie, or that set of grandkids for entirely far too long, we opted to
go spend Thanksgiving with them. Even so, I can't begin to explain the deep
sense of guilt I feel for not staying behind and spending it with Mom.

Knowing of the many ambitions and desires my Dad had not yet achieved causes me to marvel each time we speak, for he always seems to be so happy, contented, and smiles so very much.

My heart wants to believe it's because of whom he's talking to, but my spirit tells me that in addition to that, it's because that's just how good Heaven is!

December 25, 2014
China Spring, TX

> *Knowing my brother was coming for Christmas, my Mom repeatedly urged me and Pat to go spend it with Corey and his menagerie. Again, albeit reluctantly, I did just that.*
>
> *While passing out gifts and sharing some holiday thoughts, Corey explained to the kiddos how much he used to really look forward to spending Christmas with my Mom and Dad. It was then when our oldest granddaughter, Liana, smiled and said, "Yeah Daddy … just like we do with our Nana and Paw-Paw!"*
>
> *If that weren't enough to make this Christmas one to be remembered, they all sent their love and wished them both a very merry one! Liana then said that she would really like to have met them, to which I told her one day she would. She smiled and hugged me.*

Grieving and mourning are emotional tools our hearts rely upon to help soothe the pain of one's loss. Though as helpful as they may be, neither serves to answer any unresolved questions, nor provide useful directions as to our future path absent our love ones.

However, when experienced together, these recovery comrades afford us the precious time we'll need to cope with life's other demands, all the while learning to deal with something our hearts can neither handle nor yet begin to understand.

December 31, 2014
China Springs, TX
I pray this will not just be a happy new year,
but a better one for my Mom as well.

I was wondering; do you think it would help for me to pray that my prayers get answered?

I guess it wouldn't hurt, but I don't think it'll help any more than hoping it won't rain after washing my car.

December 31, 2014
China Springs, TX
Don't worry; I'm sure God also has a good sense of humor.
Happy New Year, Dad!

A New Year's Thought

Holiday seasons have a way of causing us to pray for things we know aren't really possible, but oh how our hearts wish some of them, no matter what their cost, could somehow come true.

As each new year passes, I find myself praying that the good Lord takes away half of what time remains of mine. Then, all I ask in return is that He give my Dad back to my Mom, even if it's only for such a brief … but so badly needed moment in time.

January 1, 2015
China Springs, TX
Please don't take this to be nearly as dark as it may sound. I just want everything that's possible to make what time my Mom has to be as happy as it can be.
Happy New Year to the both of you!

Just as often as good memories and pleasant thoughts help me to drift off to sleep, others abruptly awaken me to ensure that I sleep no more.

Our Lady of Wisdom
And as well they should, for not all we do and say should have been said or done.

If you find yourself hopelessly drowning in a sea of regret, what good would it do for you to reach out a helping hand to another equally afflicted?

Yet, just maybe between the two of you, together you'll survive. For being totally alone isn't surviving at all, it's merely existing, and I believe the good Lord didn't put us here just simply to exist!

Our Lady of Wisdom
Even though my Mom still doesn't really grasp where she is, she knows she's not where she wants to be … with my Dad; something I would give absolutely anything to fix.

Recollections

The Almighty has blessed us with deeply rooted thoughts, images, sounds, feelings, and even smells in the form of memories. He does this so we can instantly recall much of what has already passed, while also providing us with cherished recollections we pray to forever last.

Yet, He doesn't allow us to pick and choose the ones we get to keep or those that we'll someday lose. For He alone knows that we, as mortals, would only retain those from which we would garner even a sliver of emotional gain.

So, I've come to see where the good Lord uses memories to challenge our hearts by continually reminding us not only of what we still have, but of all that we've already lost.

My most troubling memories are of what I recall seeing in my Dad's eyes and hearing in his words not long before he passed. Now, and all too often, I'm hearing and sensing much the same futility being echoed by my Mom. What hurts almost as much is finding myself at a loss as to what I should now say or do.

Then, what can you tell someone who has lost all that there is to lose? It's not that there are no words, it's moreover that the words I'm able to conjure were never meant to convey what words alone were not meant to say.

So, tonight, I will pray that seeing her like this doesn't become yet another memory I'll come to regret or one that the Almighty has already decided as being one I shall not be allowed to ever forget.

Westlawn Cemetery
I find it odd that good memories, much like good friends,
are only considered to be good when compared
to others that are not so good.

In one's life, much is lost, never to be found or recovered.

Though some losses matter not, and some quietly slip by going both unknown and unnoticed, some are so precious that we will continue to seek them until we too become the lifelong search of yet another love one's loss.

Our Lady of Wisdom
If lately all my time, attention, and words seem to be primarily focused
upon my Mom, it's only because she's all that's been on
my mind, and I'm sure on my Dad's as well.

So, Dad ... What's Up with Mom?

With this being just a few days into the new year, I know we'd both feel a whole lot better if there was a brighter light at the end of Mom's tunnel, but like you, I'm not seeing one. And yes, I too wish it weren't true, but what little light there is appears to sadly be growing dimmer as each new day succumbs to but another.

I no longer expect to see that special twinkle in her eyes, for it's been gone as long as have you. And then, there's that grin she so proudly wears, thinking she's fooling everyone into believing she's perfectly contented just sitting there waiting for your return. However, we both know better, for what she really lives for is the day when she can join you. In that regard, I know exactly how she feels.

So, tell me; is it wrong for me to pray for something different than what she wants, or should I too be asking God to reunite the two of you? What I'm beginning to fear is that this day may not be as far away as I would prefer, or as distant as my heart earnestly prays.

Yes, I've come to accept that Mom's health clearly requires twenty-four-seven care, but that fact alone doesn't shield or insulate me from the uncertainty I see in her eyes, the insecurity I feel when we embrace, and the guilt I experience each time I must leave her. It's nonetheless as difficult as it is deeply disturbing for the both of us with its lingering stigma haunting me until I return again.

As such, I will forever continue to question my having placed her current well-being above her heart's eternal desire to have remained in her own home. It's only now that I've come to see that in trying to do what's right, I had two distinctly different paths to follow. And although you gave me a clear sign that I chose the right one, I still can't stop believing that my being right was at the cost of changing how Mom will forever after see, feel about, and think of me.

Our Lady of Wisdom
Questions of the heart seldom have really clear answers, for the
clarity we seek tends to emotionally conflict with all the
heartbreaking solutions we're unable to accept.

Irreversible Guilt

You might seriously want to take some time to think over what I'm about to share, for I truly wish I had long before my Dad's passing. The difference here is that I'm now telling you what I wish someone had told me.

So, regardless of how much we sincerely try to do, actually end up doing, or may yet need to do, some things will remain undone. However, absolutely nothing will ever be as important as that which can no longer be done ... especially for our most treasured love ones.

With that in mind, if you're ever tempted to go visit with a love one, especially those who are aging and ailing, and for whatever reason you don't, please stop whatever you're doing, realize what you're not doing, and go do what you should be doing.

With my Mom's health now declining, just the mere thought of one day no longer being able to hug, make her smile or laugh, or just simply drop by to visit, gives me more than enough reason to make this evening, and every one of her remaining tomorrows, the best they can possibly ever be.

Our Lady of Wisdom
Clearly, only God knows what the rest of today will bring,
or whatever else He might choose to take away.

Please, dear Lord, I beg of You ... take my life before You take my independence, for I've come to see what losing such did to my Dad and is now doing to my Mom.

Westlawn Cemetery
I pray for that to be neither my fate
nor my final penance.

It's not that I wish to separate the past from the present; rather, what I fear is that the past has been set on a course which has already been predestined to soon become the present.

Our Lady of Wisdom
Not until the blessing of time actually begins to close in on you will
you truly begin to appreciate just how precious time really is
and will forever be, or God forbid ... once was!

I regret my many actions and misdeeds that saddened either my Dad or Mom, and equally so for those occasions where I took them right up to disappointment's doorstep.

But because they were always willing to open the door that I sadly stood them before, I feel you can now see how and why I've come to love them all the more.

Our Lady of Wisdom
Having brought my Mom to a place she'd much rather not be, through her tired eyes
and in the depth of her sighs I'm reminded of what I prayed never to see.

I believe everyone will eventually fault themselves for not having properly conveyed to their parents how sorry they are for certain things until it's much too late to do so.

With that, some instances, hiding in the recesses of my mind, that prompted my above words, continually drive me to apologize to my Mom for how I'm now handling her current situation, for I still fear what I'm doing is wrong.

So, each time I whisper to my Dad or say outright to my Mom that I'm sorry, I feel all I'm doing is reciting but mere words that serve no good, for at this point there's no way to change or undo the damage I've already done.

Westlawn Cemetery
The faraway look I saw in my Dad's eyes, in his last few days,
I'm now beginning to see in my Mom's, and it's becoming
far more real than my heart can bear to watch.

Since dying places fewer demands upon us than did living, why do so many fear death more than life?

You think maybe it might be because they fear
where their souls might be heading!

The loss of my Dad has taught me a few life-altering lessons. More than any other is that when we're driven by either grief or regret, rational thinking has no soul, cares not, and listens not to the anguishing, tormented pleas of a surviving love one's broken heart.

It's only now that I see where begging or even praying that a love one not be taken simply serves to increase the eventual and inevitable sheer depth of our loss.

Here, once again, I find myself praying that the fear I have for all that my Mom has
yet to face is born out of concern, rather than just reality setting in.

If Not Today ... What of Tomorrow?

Every tomorrow will always have three distinct advantages over any of our todays. By tomorrow we'll know what we should or should not have done, have said or held back from saying, and ultimately, what did or did not come to pass.

Therein lies my problem; for tomorrow is sure to come, one from which I can neither hide nor try to run. Then, as today becomes tomorrow, so grows my heart's uneasy sense of impending sorrow.

So, all I can do is intensely pray that God blesses my Mom with yet another tomorrow ... and thank Him for not taking her today.

January 11, 2015
West Jefferson Hospital ~ Emergency Room
With Mom not looking or feeling too good, I had her brought to the hospital.
Although it took until really late in the evening to get her admitted,
we left only after my Dad assured me he was going to stay
with her for the rest of the night.

Never Guaranteed

Before today, whenever it came time to leave Mom, I knew I could go see her anytime I wanted to. It was just a matter of driving there, or simply turning around to go back and visit with her a bit longer.

Yet, while I was preparing to leave her today, I did so reluctantly, for I feared this might be the last time God was going to allow me to ever speak to her again, or at least not in her lifetime. This thought, or even its possibility, plagued me for the remainder of the day.

Having dealt with my Dad's death led me to realize that though we view our own as but a vague and distant reality, it's actually an ever-present companion to life itself. Yet, when all is said and done, they both become one, where life is never guaranteed, and death is the only true certainty.

January 11, 2015
West Jefferson Hospital ~ Parking Garage
With as many times as I've come to this hospital, never did I ever think
there'd be a day when this was a place I'd not want to leave.

Day 1

Not only does life repeat itself, sadly, so does death, taking with it much more than just those we love.

January 12, 2015

Oh ... That's Good!

I awoke totally confused, thinking I had overslept and was supposed to go feed my Mom's some breakfast. As I rushed into the kitchen and hastily blurted this out to Pat, she curiously asked if I didn't remember us having her admitted into the hospital yesterday and being there practically all night.

So, after I got myself to thinking a little more clearly, I called the hospital to see how she had done and if she seemed to be feeling any better this morning. Her nurse explained that she appeared to have slept really well and had just finished eating a good amount of breakfast.

When we arrived she was sleeping rather soundly. Then, at one point, while Pat and I were talking, she must have overheard us and softly asked, "Is that you, Ferdy?" "No, Mom, it's just me, but Dad's right here." She smiled and said, "Oh, that's good," and drifted back off to sleep.

Though the ensuing pages will tell the rest of the story, there's one thing it'll not explain. Hidden in amongst all the questions she asked me yesterday while in the emergency room, there's one that hovers above all else that I just can't stop thinking about.

With her having asked this same question countless times before, though under different circumstances, I should have had an answer prepared, but I didn't. For unlike before, this time a sheer sense of true hope resonated in her voice when she asked, "Hey bay, do you think maybe they might let you or Daddy take me home today?" Thankfully, before I could respond, she drifted back off to sleep. Yet, as I quietly stood next to her bed, for the umpteenth time since yesterday, I once again regretted not doing just that ... taking her back home.

It bothers me to say this, but again, I didn't answer her because I couldn't. In an odd sort of way, it was reassuring to feel my Dad encourage me to remain silent and not let a lie be the last words I'd ever speak to her. So, that's just what I did, or better said ... that's just what I didn't do.

January 12, 2015
West Jefferson Hospital ~ Room 447
I'm not so much afraid of what today might bring,
but rather ... what it has yet to take away.

No, Not Yesterday ... Sadly Today

Though my Mom had finally settled down late last night, my previous entry from this morning is clear testament that I had not, nor do I believe I will likely do so anytime soon.

Just as each time I visit with my Dad and a better part of me remains behind, so it was when I last left my Mom. However, there's a part of me that will forever wish I had, in fact, remained and eternally regret that I didn't.

As far as she's concerned, she was in just another room, in just another hospital, and it was yet just another day that hopefully brought her closer to going home, the place where she wanted to be and truly belonged. I still can't help but feel that it's my fault she'd not where she should be.

After rereading and rethinking what I had written yesterday, it's only now that I see where God was clearly trying to prepare me, through my own words, for what it appeared He may have already planned for her later today.

I found myself praying for her to awaken so we could talk, or I could at least let her know I was there. Yet, she looks so tired and the fight she's fought so bravely has all but worn her down; she needed to rest. It was then when my Dad quietly let me know that it's time to start praying for what's best for Mom, rather than how my worried heart wants it to be.

In hindsight, though the efforts and messages of both the Almighty and my Dad were more than clear, they knew I was not yet prepared to face what lay ahead. So, for reasons that need not be explained, I turned a deafened ear to what my tormented soul neither wanted to know nor could bear to hear.

January 12, 2015
West Jefferson Hospital ~ Room 447
These last few days I've spent with my Mom has shown me what it had to have been like for her as she sat, watch, and tearfully waited as the Almighty finally decided what He was going to do with my Dad. And then, to have agonized over exactly when did He intend to do it.

The Last and Final Call

After I spent the better part of the day visiting with Mom, one of her nurses came to let me know the hospital pharmacy didn't have one of her eye medications. So, I offered to go retrieve some from her nursing home.

Right before I left, Mom had gone back to sleep, so I opted not to wake her. I thought surely later this evening we'd have plenty time to talk, bid each other good night, and I could tell her I love her, but again, I was so very wrong and at such a critical time.

While I was returning to the hospital, Pat called to see where I was. The crackling of her voice let me know she wasn't asking this for anyone's benefit but my own. Though she tried her best, she was unable to hide her anguish or fear. And having heard that combination of immediacy and deep distress in her voice only once before, I knew if I didn't hurry, I might repeat a mistake I both prayed and promised never to make! Believe me, the number of corners I cut, and how I got back to the hospital so quickly, truly had to have been a combination of my Dad directing me and sheer divine intervention.

Then, while I was getting into the elevator, Pat called again to check on my location and in less than a minute later, she called once more. This time the urgency of her words was clear and to the point. As I turned down the corridor, all I could see was Pat frantically waving her hands in a way that conveyed what her words couldn't say.

So, if you don't mind, I'd like to talk with just my Mom:

(Continued)

I now see where Pat's sense of dread was mixed with a sad, conflicting sense of relief. Though she too felt she was about to lose you, the past sixteen-plus years have made her painfully aware of just how much my not being with Dad when he passed has continued to haunt me. So, she knew how very much it meant for me to be with you when it came time for you to leave.

As I approached your bedside, you were lying there so still and quiet. Although you didn't look as rested, it was comforting to see you were no longer in any pain. At Dad's urging, I told you, "Hey, Mom, I'm back ... I'm here."

Just as those words left my lips you took a shallow but quite pronounced breath, as if to let me know you'd heard me. I glanced up at your nurse, who clearly sensed my concern and reassured me that you were still with us. At that point, Pat put her arm around me and tearfully tried to explain how she could clearly tell you had been waiting for me to return.

With forever regretting not being able to tell Dad goodbye or express my love for him just before he passed, I was determined to not let that happen with you. So, I gently placed my hand upon your shoulder, leaned over, kissed your forehead, and told you I love you. I pray you'll remember my doing that for as long as will I.

Then, within a mere second or two, you took one final, short breath. Pat hugged me once again and tried her best to comfort me by telling me, "You see, I told you she waited." I remember thinking how I wished your last breath to instead have been that of mine. It was then when I could feel Dad's spirit embracing yours, and the two of you were then reunited forevermore.

Well, it wasn't until later when Pat helped me recall my last moments with you that I learned I had also told you it was okay to let go because Dad was right there waiting for you. I now see where he had me speak those final words to you not just for your benefit, but for mine as well.

January 12, 2015
West Jefferson Hospital ~ Room 447 / 4:30 pm
Though we left entirely too much unsaid and undone, we now have till the end of time to make up for all those lost times. And by the way, with this being Dad's birthday, the two of you can finally celebrate it together, and not only today ... but for the rest of forever!
Happy Birthday, Dad! Please give Mom a big hug for me.

Continuing conversations with my Dad and now, I pray … with my Mom as well.

Shirley (Melling) Perrien 1925 – 2015
[Photo circa 1946]

Together my Dad and Mom somehow managed to both guide and inspire me up to, through, and beyond this point. May they rest in peace … or at least until I get there!

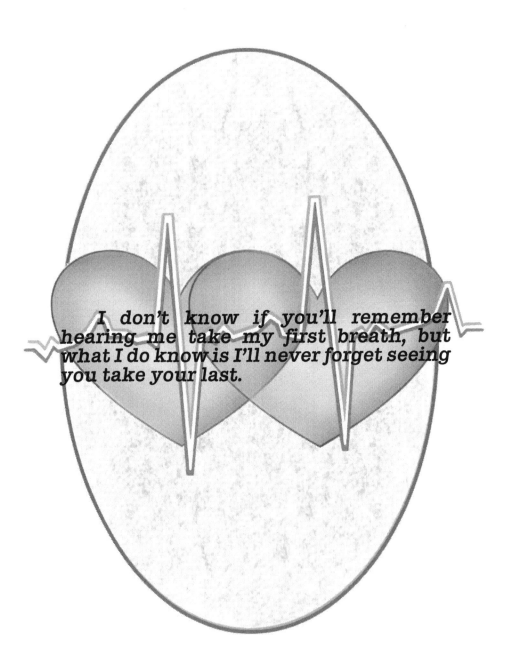

I don't know if you'll remember hearing me take my first breath, but what I do know is I'll never forget seeing you take your last.

Just As With My Dad

A short while ago, when the sheer reality of my Mom's passing finally sunk in, my first feelings were of wanting to leave with her ... just as with my Dad.

Then, my less virtuous acts as a youngster served as kindling to restoked the flames of my ongoing fear that I'll be made to suffer her absence too ... just as with my Dad.

Clearly, I dread the thought of where I might be made to go, for where eternal flames fill an unholy place and blessed reunions with love ones are never bestowed. Yet, by staying behind there might be a slight chance the Almighty will allow ongoing talks with my Mom to be had ... just as with my Dad.

So, maybe my not being allowed to leave won't be all that sad, especially if things turn out with my Mom ... just as with my Dad.

January 12, 2015
Over time, a relationship with my Dad has evolved into what you've read thus far.
I pray that this very same evolution soon takes place with my Mom as well.

The Sad Truth

All of my good deeds, manicured words, endless string of righteous promises, and heartfelt prayers could not stop or even delay what happened today.

Yet, the one thing that is different, which I see to be a good thing, is that my Mom no longer has to worry or repeatedly ask, "So, how's Daddy doing?" for she can now and forevermore after ask this of him ... herself!

January 12, 2015
What a lady once told me at the cemetery, "I shouldn't feel so bad about leaving since the better part of my heart remains behind" applies ... yet once again today.

Being there to watch my Mom leave truly doesn't make it any easier to believe, or even accept that I won't get to see her again until she and my Dad are both standing there waiting for that blessed day when I can then join them.

January 12, 2015
Though my Dad and I continue to converse, just the mere thought of having that same spiritual bond with my Mom gives me something to truly look forward to.
So, until I feel her words also echoing in my heart, I will just have to live with what I pray to be her temporary silence.

Happy Birthday, Dad

You may think it odd for me to be wishing my Dad a Happy Birthday with my Mom having just passed away.

However, what you may not understand is that now and ever after, not only can we celebrate his birthday, but we can also rejoice in knowing that today was the day God granted both of their greatest wishes. He brought the two of them back together, but this time He made sure it was but the first day of forever after.

January 12, 2015
Well above all the pain and sorrow now filling my heart, I must
thank God for no longer keeping my Mom and Dad apart!

Try as We May

Before the first tear falls, I assure you, you'll find yourself trying to tell a departed love one just how much you love them. And no matter how hard you try, only then will you come to learn the true value of but a single word that can no longer be heard.

If by the time a love one passes and they've yet to feel the true depth and sincerity of your love, trying to fill that void after the fact will be but yet another disappointing exercise in the reality of death.

You're also likely to catch yourself repeating how much you're going to miss them, or that you don't know how you're ever going to live without them. At that point you'll boldly proclaim to the Almighty that there's absolutely nothing you wouldn't do just to embrace them, even if but only once again. And yes, I can confess this to you because as you've previously read … I did all of this and even more.

Try as we may, when mortals say or do things long after we should have, though well intended, such past-due emotional fences are never fully mended. It's during these times when we must rely upon our kindred spirits to converse on our behalf. For while they're busy talking, nothing else should be said or heard, other than the beating of two devoted hearts declaring their life-long passion for each other through never-ending, ever-loving words.

January 12, 2015
Obviously, my Dad's birthday was always a day to be remembered, but never
did I ever think it would also be for this. God finally decided it was
time to give him that one special gift no one else could!

With my Dad's passing I've come to fear death no more, yet, having just lost my Mom I oddly find myself welcoming it like never before.

Please don't take me wrong, for I truly wish not to die, at least not right here and now. Then, again, knowing what's soon to follow, it's probably best you not ask this of me come later today and surely not tomorrow.

January 12, 2015
No matter how many love ones have passed, each feels no different than the first.

Within seconds of losing love ones our sense of time and reality immediately evaporate only to be replaced with feelings of sorrow, regret, grief, and total disbelief.

Time will swiftly become all-consuming simply by consuming all there is.

January 12, 2015
As with my Dad's passing, I'll manage to somehow get through this,
but this time I'll have him here to help me along the way.

The Blame Game

Too often, in the past, I blamed the many things I would or should have done differently by using the well-worn and equally inexcusable excuse "Had I only known." It's become obvious to me that each time I said so, I unknowingly laid bare both my sheer ignorance and unspoken shame.

By professing what I claim to not have known, all I was really doing was trying to disguise all that I did know but failed to acknowledge. Clearly, I did so simply to avoid the blame and pain for not having been the son I should have been, especially when that's all my Mom and Dad ever really needed me to be.

January 12, 2015
Well, it's time for the two of you to go celebrate both Mom's
arrival and Dad's birthday. And please ... keep in touch!

Rightfully so, neither sorrow nor does one's loss have any boundaries or limitations.

January 12, 2015
More than just the end to this day has come and gone.

In His infinite wisdom, God not only saw to it that
my Mom and Dad stayed together for the
better part of their lives, He's brought
them back together … forever.

My Mom and Dad
[Photo circa 1944]

Even through tear-filled eyes it's so plain to see
how the Almighty knew long ago this was
the way it was always meant to be.

Thank You!

For those who may have flipped to this page simply by chance, my words will likely have little meaning nor pose any real consequence. And if you haven't already read any of what I've written, what concern would you have as to what I've yet to write? If that's so, might I suggest you thumb back a page or two, where the sincerity of my words might entice you to read more than just those few. Who knows, you may very well come to see how my transcribed thoughts and feelings were written as much for you as they ever were for me.

With all that I've written, I didn't think composing a closing would have presented all that much of a problem, but it has. The mere fact that it's literally taken me years since my Dad and Mom's passing to embrace and come to terms with the very idea of drawing this to a close, albeit a temporary one, became all too real. My hesitancy stands as a testament to the challenge doing so posed to both my heart and pen. So, how was I to cease doing what I didn't want to end?

Well, at first, I took the easy way out and just continued doing what I had become so accustomed to. Then, the more time passed, the more I began to fear that our collective words, thoughts, and emotions would eventually become lost in some old, nondescript computer file. They would then slowly fade away along with my equally aging mind. Clearly, I truly didn't want all of this to become just another of the many things this old foolish soul might regretfully leave behind.

If it's my destiny to be but a simple scribe for my Dad and Mom, then so be it. Believe me, it'll please me beyond my ability to describe if I do nothing more than continue to convey all they have yet to say. Their spirits, while taking refuge in my pen, demand I do precisely as our three hearts dictate.

Way back in the very beginning of my journey I asked if my words served to comfort or inspire you to view love, life, and yes, even death somewhat differently, to let me know how and why. Then, if I somehow managed to move you to better appreciate not only the love ones you still have but those who've passed on, again ... please let me know of this as well.

Let there be no doubt; it's your friendship and respect that I absolutely treasure the most. So, please, as I've previously requested, feel free to write and reach out to me ... just as often as you wish at:

TheAginCajun@GaryPerrien.com

A Passing Thought

I often find myself thinking
of all the amazing wildflowers
that thrived in vast open fields or
behind old abandoned barns only
to sadly die ... all alone.

Though they flourished so bright
and beautifully, they were never to
be seen or ever so much as enjoy an
admiring passing glance.

With absolutely no mistaken conceit
intended nor the slightest implied, I
beg a similar scenario not to become
the fate of this *Agin' Cajun* as well.

I truly look forward to sharing a
lot more time and words with you.
So, until then, my equally troubled
friend, take care, and absolutely
by all means ... keep in touch!

Ain't No Way, LLC

I've been repeatedly asked by more than just a few as to how this "Ain't No Way, LLC" on the Copyright page came to be. So, for those of you who are as curious as are my dear friends, let me put all of your inquiring minds to rest. And because those three nondescript words came about as uniquely as did most of my other phrasings, here's the story behind their place in time.

On April 14, 1999, once again I found myself in the Dallas airport. To pass the time, I began proofreading some of what I had written one year ago, on the day of my Dad's passing. Well, apparently, the gentleman sitting next to me had been reading what I had thus far edited, as I laid the finished pages across the arm that separated our chairs. At one point, he remarked something to the effect, "Now that one's really good!" Because his words were clearly spoken in my direction, I replied, "So, I take it you like that one. I can move them if they're in your way?" He quickly responded, "No, please don't," and went on to make a few additional favorable comments. He then asked if I was an editor or something, and if so, who did I work for? I couldn't help but chuckle before explaining that I was my own editor and that all of these were my writings. He then said, "Oh, really, I didn't get to read all of them, but the parts I did are really nice; some are quite touching." I thanked him and began packing up my stuff as our plane was preparing to start boarding.

As he too gathered his belongings, he asked if I had any intentions on ever publishing "my stuff," to which I hastily replied that one day I hope to. Without hesitation he abruptly fired back, "Well, good luck with that! People like us don't get those kinds of breaks." The only thing my disappointed heart could think to say was "Really!" Then, as he headed toward the boarding gate, he ended our conversation with, "Yeah, ain't no way ... but I wish you the best of luck."

Because I had everything packed, including my phone, I couldn't jot down or even dictate a recorded note as to what he had just said. So, instead, I kept repeating "ain't no way" to myself the whole time I was boarding. Once I got seated, I wrote those very words in bold capital letters across the first page in my binder. With it being the anniversary of my Dad's passing, both he and my heart told me that one day I'd figure out a way to use this stranger's ominous comment to give some kind of unique meaning or twist to my words. So, when it came time to pick a name for the business through which I would later publish my writings, needless to say, it could only be ... "Ain't No Way!"

Sorry, but if you'll please indulge me ... I have a few closing thoughts to just my Mom and Dad.

Though I've tried my best to meaningfully express what your presence and passing has meant to me, I still see where my words alone can't begin to mend that which has no fix, nor a foreseeable end.

Albeit completely futile and entirely too late, I've come to appreciate the two of you so much more than I ever did before. And although I know the Almighty is never revengeful, I can't help but wonder if my many past failings may be why He's chosen to admonish me so.

On the one hand, He lifts my soul by allowing our spirits to openly and freely speak, but then, on the other, He leaves me with limp and empty arms with which I'm unable to embrace you following our many spiritual encounters.

As such, my mourning causes me to wear many faces as I grieve and lament over your absence. Even in spite of what I know can't come to be, I still seek your presence in my prayers each night and with practically every idle thought.

And though my eyes and thoughts may, at times, become distracted and cast in different directions, please know that my heart will always be looking upward ... at the two of you.

Your loving son...

If you've taken some comfort from what I've tried to say and do, please consider sharing my words with others.

Though you might find this to be an odd request, but if there are others close to you that you feel could garner some consolation or even gain a sense of emotional release from my words, I'd be forever grateful if you'd simply just lend them your copy. If you choose to do so, please encourage them to read it thoroughly ... with an open mind, and thoughtfully ... with an open heart.

However, if you wish not to part with your copy, please consider getting another so you can lend it to your friends. And be sure to ask them that once they're finished, they too continue passing it around.

If you didn't just flip to this page and have, instead, read up to this point, I believe my words will have clearly shown that what motivates me is far from the sale of my book. If, through you and but one other copy I can move the hearts of untold others, that would be more than payment enough.

Also, you could post some thoughts on your Facebook page directing your friends to my book before heading over to mine where you could post your comments on which of my words or thoughts moved you the most. And oh yeah, if you would, please don't forget to reach out to me via my email to let me know of both your thoughts and actions.

And last but certainly not least, I can't begin to thank you enough for opting to take this long and heart wrenching journey with me. I can only pray that by having traveled such similar agonizing paths we've become life-long companions where our hearts will forever remain together and look forward to future journeys ... wherever they may eventually lead us.

TheAginCajun@GaryPerrien.com

To Be Continued

Whenever we speak, we tend to reveal what we want others to know, think, hear, or even believe. However, when we write, an entirely different side of us comes through. Quite boldly, our pen lays bare more of our true self than our spoken words could ever possibly disclose.

I will forever have a special place in my heart for all the loving souls who've hung in and traveled this entire journey with me, suffering and rejoicing along the way. Though destiny may have brought us together, it was through our mutual pain we became one and the same; with our shared loss bonding our hearts, together we will forever remain.

Long before my Mom passed, I knew if I didn't pause what I was doing my wish to share this with you would never have come to fruition. Yet, every time I tried to place a period upon what was evolving into a never-ending sentence, neither my heart nor my pen was willing to give up or give in.

The question I'm asked the most is how do I find words that define another's pain simply by reliving that of mine? Well, my answer is and has always been what I now offer to you. When our pain is the same, placing the words upon the page becomes the easy part. What's so hard is experiencing such mutually troubling thoughts, and then openly capturing what's silently eating away at our equally confused and aching hearts.

The only thing I can do now is offer you a brief introduction to a really long overdue intermission. Though my Mom's passing place an menacing detour along my journey; it was but another sign, as clear as the one that got me to this place in time, for it left me with no doubt that you, my pen, and my aching heart all needed a belated timeout.

No matter how hard I've struggled to breathe life into my words, it won't be until you feel and experience the depth of what I've tried to say will they too have a reason to live. Whether you believe me to be right or wrong is not as important as it is for you to simply accept, as I've said before, that it's okay to be wrong ... if it's for all the right reasons.

Like you, I too know not when my own divine time will arrive. As such, I pray each day that my allotted span not come to its end, or at least not as long as my words continue to move others' hearts and my aging hand can still hold a pen. Trust me, I truly have a lot more to offer, just not here or now.

With that said, I can think of no better words or thought to leave you with than the very ones I last spoke to my Dad, and now tearfully feel driven to utter to both my Mom and you as well ... "I'll see ya' later!"

So, please take care, my friend...
until we meet again!

Made in the USA
Coppell, TX
02 January 2020

13996115R00125